Make your dreams come true

The *art* of *wish*-practice in *8 steps*

U L L I   S P R I N G E T T

PIATKUS

Visit the Piatkus website!

Piatkus publishes a wide range of bestselling fiction and non-fiction, including books on health, mind, body & spirit, sex, self-help, cookery, biography and the paranormal.

If you want to:
- read descriptions of our popular titles
- buy our books over the Internet
- take advantage of our special offers
- enter our monthly competition
- learn more about your favourite Piatkus authors

VISIT OUR WEBSITE AT: www.piatkus.co.uk

© 2002 Ulli Springett

First published in 2002 by
Judy Piatkus (Publishers) Ltd
5 Windmill Street, London W1T 2JA

The moral rights of the author have been asserted

A catalogue record for this book is available from the British Library

ISBN 0-7499-2339-3

Phototypeset by Action Publishing Technology, Gloucester
Printed & bound in Great Britain by
Antony Rowe Ltd, Chippenham

Contents

About the author

Ulli Springett is the author of *Symbol Therapy* and *How To Find Your Soulmate*. She would be delighted to hear about your results with wish-practice and can be contacted for workshops and talks, care of Piatkus Books, 5 Windmill Street, London W1T 2JA or via e-mail: ulli@holistic-health.uk.com Please visit her website at www.authorpages.co.uk/ullispringett

Acknowledgements

As always I wish to express my deepest gratitude to my Buddhist teachers Shenpen Hookham, Rigdzin Shikpo and His Eminence Garchen Rinpoche. You are the beacons of my life and my only true refuge. Thank you to my soulmate and husband Nigel, who shares and supports my journey in every respect. Without your generosity this book would not have been written. And Richard, thank you very much for your friendship, support and enthusiasm.

Introduction

Do you know what a wish-fulfilling gem is?

It is a beautiful, brilliant jewel that has a fantastic quality: it can make your wishes come true. When you take a wish-fulfilling gem between your palms and press it lightly to your heart you just need to utter your wish with conviction and faith and it will only be a matter of time until your desire will be fulfilled. Wouldn't it be nice to possess such a wonderful gem? Wouldn't you give *anything* to possess it?

Well, here comes some very good news: everybody, yes, everybody possesses such a wish-fulfilling gem and has the ability to make their wishes come true. The jewel that can transform your desires into reality is actually your own heart and its innermost qualities. You might not yet believe it, but if you become aware that you possess this wonderful treasure, you can realise your most spectacular dreams.

I am not talking from theory; my own life is proof of what I am saying. I have transformed from somebody who was very miserable into someone who is constantly saying, 'I am sooo happy! I have everything in life I could possibly wish for.'

What happened?

I began to learn how I could make my dreams come true through a method called wish-practice in my early twenties. I started to work more systematically with this method in my early thirties, after which time my difficult life changed dramatically. I got rid of all my problems one by one. My relationships skills, which were near zero, transformed so fundamentally that I can now claim to have the most wonderful, loving and inspiring relationships that I can think of. From being totally disinterested in work and underachieving I have changed to someone who is successful. And, what is even more important, I love my work so much that it's more like a passion that I can't get enough of. I have been very poor – scratching and scrimping for every penny – and this area has changed like everything else in my life.

Let me tell you just one of my stories. When I first started to write books the odds for my getting published weren't very high. My mother tongue is German and I had lived in England for just two years when I endeavoured to be a published author. My English was good enough to go shopping and to read the bus timetable but certainly not developed enough to be an author. I couldn't even follow the films on television! I can just imagine how people must have inwardly smiled at me and my 'unrealistic' dreams to be a successful writer.

And, yes, if I hadn't known about wish-practice, if I had been a 'sensible' person, I wouldn't even have tried. But I knew about my wish-fulfilling gem – so I was undeterred. I wrote two books and my aim was to be published with one particular, well-known publisher. I was told that it was highly unlikely I would be taken on as a newcomer but I tried it nevertheless and out of the blue help appeared.

A friend of mine turned out to be an English teacher for foreigners and he generously offered to edit my books. In the beginning he found an average of eighty(!) mistakes per page and with an enormous effort he corrected the whole lot. But that was not enough. He was also very interested in the content of my books, discussed and explored them with me and put all the exercises enthusiastically into practice. Both of my books were published shortly afterwards and one of them with exactly the publisher I had wished for. All that happened within less than two years.

Maybe I have just been lucky. But maybe these are the results of wish-practice.

How did I come to this point?

I have been a dedicated practitioner of Tibetan Buddhism for seventeen years and I had the luck to find qualified and helpful teachers. Wish-practice is an acknowledged Buddhist practice, which I learnt from my Buddhist teachers, Shenpen Hookham and Rigdzin Shikpo. I have also been a psychotherapist for fourteen years. For the first seven years I worked mainly with gestalt therapy and family therapy, but then I moved on to work with transpersonal methods, which include the spiritual side of a client, and these methods brought results at a *much* faster rate.

I have always felt fascinated by the challenge to make spiritual insight so practical that *anybody* can use it to solve their own personal problems, be they psychological, physical or even financial in nature. Transpersonal psychotherapy is one way of doing this; wish-practice is another.

However, I felt that in order to use and integrate the Buddhist method of wish-practice into my own life and into that of my clients it needed some additional psychological techniques. Wish-practice is a highly spiritual and effective method, but if you lack psychological know-how it can be difficult to harvest the results from this wonderful tool.

Because I was so fascinated by wish-practice and wanted really big changes for myself, I dedicated my life to make wish-practice work for the averagely confused person (like myself). In the end I came up with eight steps, which take into account all kinds of possible obstacles and hang-ups and how to overcome them. With these eight steps you can change your life in the same way that I, and everybody else to whom I have taught this method, have changed our lives. You can work on all areas of your life, the spiritual, the psychological and the material, and bring about fantastic results.

Everybody can work with wish-practice, no matter what kind of spiritual path they follow or whether they are religious at all. I have taught wish-practice to many of my clients and it was wonderful to see them evolving. You don't need to sit for hours in meditation, nor do you need to be an expert in psychological matters. In fact, in order to be successful with wish-practice you only need one, single attitude and that is a whole-hearted and deep belief that your wish will come true. 'Ouch,' you might say, 'then I might as well give it up right from the start because I can't imagine how I could possibly believe that my dreams will come true.'

Wait a minute, and I will offer you a way to learn to believe in the unbelievable. The way to do this is to work with symbols that are given to you by your own Higher Consciousness. By visualising these symbols for just two minutes a day you will experience how your doubts and anxieties will melt away and are replaced by trust and conviction that your wish will come true. This exercise is part of symbol therapy for wish-practice, which will help you to get over any obstacle you might encounter while trying to bring your dream into existence.

Wish-practice has eight major steps. The first four will tell you what to do and the other four will tell you what *not* to do. You begin by finding your heart-wish. Before you start dedicating yourself to a wish it is a good idea to be very sure that this wish will bring you real happiness once it is fulfilled. Step 1 of wish-practice will tell you how you can find those wishes.

Step 2 will teach you how you can strengthen the wish-power of your heart-mind and you will learn how to use your entire spiritual and mental power to attract what you want.

In Step 3 you have to work for your wish skilfully, with your purpose in mind.

Then you can move on to Step 4, which will explain to you how you can raise your own vibration. This means becoming happier and more content, even though your wish isn't fulfilled yet. This sounds more difficult than it is and I will show you exactly how you can achieve it.

In Step 5 you will learn how to let go of your craving. For impatient people (like myself) Step 5 can be quite a challenge, so I will give you plenty of methods to master it successfully.

Then you can go on to Step 6, which will explain to you how to deal with the unavoidable waiting time and possible setbacks.

Step 7 deals with any remaining obstacles. If you are lucky you will no longer have any bigger obstacles and you can move right on to the final and best bit of wish-practice, Step 8: receiving your wish without making bad compromises!

Throughout the book you will find quite a few practical exercises, which are all tried and proven and completely safe. If you just read them you can learn a lot about the theory of wish-practice. But if you want to make your own wishes come true, I am afraid you have to *do* them. However, because I know that some readers of self-help books are reluctant to do any exercises I have tried to make them as short and simple as possible so that you can do them almost as fast as you could read them.

There is only one exercise, called the 'wish-practice method', which you will have to do on a regular basis in an undisturbed place. It is explained in Step 2 and will take just fifteen minutes each day. You can even do this exercise while lying in bed before you go to sleep. In that way, I believe, nobody should be able to say that wish-practice has asked too much of their time.

In any case, once you get into this method and you have achieved your first successes you will spend this time quite happily because you know that it will help you to make the most impossible dreams come true.

Our wishes can come true and they do come true. It is important to warn people about this and tell them to be really careful about what they want because they *will* get it one day. But most people don't believe it, and they carelessly wish for this and that on the basis of their very limited beliefs of what is possible. When these kinds of wishes come true the results can be quite devastating.

Let me tell you W.W. Jacobs's startling story of the monkey's paw, which illustrates this point quite nicely:

> Once upon a time a family, named White, was given a monkey's paw by an old friend. This monkey's paw, the friend said, had the ability to grant them three wishes. But he warned them as well and implied that there was a mysterious danger involved in making these wishes. He advised the family to throw the paw away. But the Whites did not heed his advice and father White wished at once for a large amount of money. Then the whole family went to bed and the next day they had almost forgotten about the funny monkey's paw and their wish for money.
>
> In the late afternoon a stranger appeared on their doorstep with a grave face. He brought Mr and Mrs White the dreadful news that their son had died at work in a terrible accident. As a compensation, the stranger said, the company would give them a generous sum of money. It turned out that it was exactly the amount that father White had wished for the evening before. Mr and Mrs White were numb with pain and fell into a deep depression.
>
> Ten days later Mrs White suddenly sat up in bed with a loud cry. 'The monkey's paw,' she yelled, 'we've still got two wishes!' She convinced her reluctant husband to use the paw again to wish their son alive. And so he did.

A few hours later there was a quiet knock at the door. Their son had returned, but now he was a terrible monster looking for revenge. The father used the monkey's paw for the third time and successfully wished the monster away.

This story brings home the message that we have to be very careful and wise with our wishes if we want them to make us and the people around us really happy. This insight is in total alignment with Buddhism, which tells us that we ourselves have actually created our entire life through nothing other than our own beliefs and wishes and the ways we acted upon them. But many of us find that hard to believe and we can't see the connection between our earlier wishes and our present problems. When destiny strikes out against us or when we don't have what we want we just feel at the mercy of a random and unfair universe. However, if we can accept that all our present problems have been created through our unwise wishes in the past we can develop the motivation to make our present wishes in a more intelligent way.

Wish-practice is the art of learning to use the power of our wish-fulfilling gem in a way that leads to *real* happiness. It is the art of developing so much wisdom and insight that we can create a future that is much more satisfying than our present life.

The most important ingredient in finding deep happiness and fulfilment is to make your wishes with an altruistic motivation. You don't have to give up anything you want; you just need to have the motivation to contribute with your own personal desires to the well-being of others. Then and only then will you be able to create the wonderful life that you are looking for. The eight steps of wish-practice described in this book will tell you exactly how you can make your dreams come true.

How Does Wish-practice Work?

How is it possible to call things into existence with the power of your mind? How can you make things happen that none of your friends thought were possible?

In order to get the most out of the eight steps of wish-practice it is important to have a clear understanding of the enormous power of your mind and its ability to 'create reality'. This understanding will deepen your trust in case the going gets a bit tough and it will help you to correct any wrong attitude that might hinder the process.

The best way to understand wish-practice is to think of a dream. While we are dreaming we usually don't have the slightest doubt that our dream experience is real. We are chased by dream-monsters and we are frightened to death; we meet somebody nice and we are delighted. Only when we wake up do we know that all this wasn't true. Now imagine that you become aware that you are dreaming while you are still fast asleep. If you knew that all that you experienced was a dream you wouldn't be frightened any more of the monsters, would you? On the contrary, if you knew that your experience was a self-created dream you would try to change it into something wonderful so that you could indulge in the fulfilment of your deepest wishes.

Now imagine that your whole life is created by your unconscious mind just like a dream. In fact it is a dream! You are dreaming right now while you are reading this book. No? How do you know? If you think carefully, you will find that there is no way to prove that you are not dreaming at the moment.

Our so-called reality is no more real than a dream.

If you find such a thought disconcerting think for a moment about the wonderful implications of this if it were right. If our existence is no more real than a dream then we don't need to be afraid any more and we could change everything in our lives that is dull and horrid.

I find this a wonderful idea. In fact, since it has dawned on me that our 'reality' is not as real as I thought I have started to have lucid dreams. In a lucid dream one realises that one dreams without waking up. As a result I often 'change' my dream-experience into something that suits me better. If, for example, I have a nightmare and I realise that it is just a dream I just 'will' it to become more pleasant. It always works but I am far from being a master in these kinds of things. My Buddhist teachers do much more meaningful things in their lucid dreams, like visiting enlightened beings and receiving teachings from them. But nobody is perfect!

The way I change my night-dreams mirrors the way I 'change' my life. I just assume it isn't more real than a dream and I 'will' it into something that suits me better. I have been quite successful in doing this and I am not the kind of person who is easy to please. On the contrary, I am not at all adaptable and I find it nearly impossible to put up with things that go against my grain. Being sensitive and vulnerable by nature I have very high expectations of the people around me and I want everything always to be in a beautiful and loving harmony. But, you see, even for someone as demanding as me, there is hope. If I can create a wonderful life for myself, you can as well.

THE PRIMORDIAL GROUND FROM WHICH EVERYTHING ARISES

My Buddhist teachers have explained that everything is, at its deepest level, space. This space is called the primordial ground, and it is not dead and empty but bright and beautiful and pregnant with possibilities. It is inherently good and has a living and deeply loving quality. Anything we experience in this universe has arisen from this primordial ground – physical things, people, animals, thoughts, emotions and anything else. Even the negative and bad things come from this space. However, the primordial ground in itself remains good and untouched by any negativity. It is by separating themselves from the love and goodness of this space that people become bad.

One way of looking at the primordial ground is to see it as unformed and loving potentiality, which is at the basis of everything that exists or will exist in this universe. Things arise from this potentiality and manifest in the 'real' world, and when they die and cease to exist they go back to this space.

If we can get in touch with the pure and loving qualities of the primordial space we will see that it is also at the core of ourselves and that it is our true nature. It is our Higher Consciousness and can be found in our heart and its innermost qualities of love and wisdom, and can be experienced directly in the form of blissful, compassionate awareness. But it can equally manifest in the form of enlightened beings that surround us with their love and goodness and guide us along our way.

The primordial ground is our Higher Consciousness from which everything arises that exists in the universe.

A direct experience of our Higher Consciousness is the most wonderful thing, and our deep longings for freedom, peace and loving harmony are in fact desires to go back to our primordial home – to the space that is the mother of everything and ourselves. If we can do this fully we have overcome all suffering and we are enlightened.

However, no matter how much we long to become one with the primordial ground, we feel equally driven away and threatened by it because we wrongly perceive it as representing boredom, loneliness and monotony. The amount of duties, entertainment and busy occupation we pile into our lives is a barometer that shows how much we experience the primordial ground as a threat rather than seeing its wonderful qualities.

The nearest most of us get to the experience of our Higher Consciousness are moments of intense happiness and love. In these short moments normal boundaries disappear and give way to something bigger than our usual sense of who we are. But although we enjoy these states of bliss we don't really want to lose ourselves too much, so we are trying to recapture our sense of our normal self, and as we do so the love and happiness we experience are reduced to a 'manageable' amount and finally disappear. (It could be said that this process of wanting to be in control explains the cause of all human misery.)

But all is not lost, even if we can't experience the primordial ground fully. There is a way to come nearer to it and to influence what arises from it. That is what wish-practice is about.

INFLUENCING THE PRIMORDIAL GROUND WITH OUR WILL-POWER

According to Buddhist teachings it is actually possible to determine and influence with the will-power of our heart-mind what arises from the primordial ground. And, through this technique, the teachers say, we can make our deepest wishes come true.

There are three main ways to influence the primordial ground. The first is through concentration, the second is through love and the third is through sound.

Concentration

Concentration works like a magnifying glass that can ignite a fire when it is held up to the sun. When you concentrate on something for long enough with the firm belief that it will come true it has a strong tendency to manifest in just the way you imagined it.

For example, if you always think and believe that you are a loser and unlucky with lovers it is unlikely that you will ever find a great job and a wonderful partner. But if you unwaveringly believed from an early age that you would become famous one day, the odds are you will be. If you can sit like an accomplished yogi in deep samadhi with a 100 per cent focused mind you could manifest things quite quickly.

Love

Not everybody can meditate like an advanced yogi and luckily there is an easier way to influence the primordial space and that is through love. When you feel the love in your heart you are closer in touch with your deepest being, which is in essence the primordial space itself, and in that way you are much more able to influence it. In wish-practice we use love in two ways. On the one hand we just love what we want, which is obviously not very difficult. On the other hand we have to develop an attitude of altruistic love, which means wanting to benefit other beings with our wish. Altruistic love makes us beautifully magnetic and helps us to attract what we want. Even better, whatever we are trying to 'love into existence' will definitely make us happy once it has manifested, because whatever we give out will come back to us. When we use love to make our wishes come true only love and happiness will come back.

Sound

You are probably familiar with the third way to influence the primordial ground from these words in the Bible. They start, 'In the beginning was the word ...' and then God created the world. So God uses the power of sound to create reality. Buddhist teachings agree that sound is at the very basis of creation and we will put this insight into practice through the use of a powerful declaration to the universe.

What is lost in some Christian contexts is the knowledge that we are all divine in our very nature, that God and humanity are not separate and that we are all continuously' creating reality just like God. Wish-practice is the art that makes this process of creation more conscious, so that it will lead to happiness rather than to suffering.

After all this theory it is time to try some practice. The first exercise deals with the wish to become happier.

Exercise
First Experience of Wish-practice

*Do this once

- Examine how you are feeling overall right now. If feeling extremely bad is zero and feeling extremely good is ten, where are you at the moment?

- Now try to recall one of the happiest moments of your life. Tell yourself about all the details of this happy time and relish the memory. Do this for at least two minutes.

• Stay in your memory and measure again where you are on the scale. In all likelihood your well-being will have risen at least one or two points.

• Ask yourself: where has this increased well-being come from?

There are many possible answers to this question. You could say, for example, that your increased well-being comes from your positive memory. But where did these thoughts come from? From your brain? You could say, 'My good feelings come from the chemicals and electrical impulses in my brain.' But where do these chemicals and impulses come from? From your thoughts? That puts us in a chicken-and-egg situation.

The answer is that your positive thoughts and feelings have arisen from the primordial ground, which is our highest and innermost consciousness. What you have just experienced was a short and simple form of successful wish-practice. In that little exercise you went through all the points and ingredients that are necessary to make your wishes come true. That wasn't so difficult, was it?

Looking at the exercise a little bit more closely, the first step is to make your wish (that was the wish to be happier). In the second step you need to focus on your wish or to love it. (I think most people love to feel happier.) Then you need some skilful action to make your wish come true (focusing on a happy memory), which is the third step. However, wish-practice only works if you are able to let go of trying to control the process (I hope that you were distracted enough by this exercise, so that you didn't control the process too much) and *Voila!* a miracle appears – happiness descends on you out of nowhere.

It really was a miracle, even though this was just a simple little exercise. You didn't take your increased happiness out of a drawer in your bedroom where it was safely stored for your miserable days. Happiness, like anything else in the universe, appears out of nowhere, out of the primordial, loving space that can give birth to anything. By doing this exercise you have been skilful enough to lure it into existence – congratulations!

WANTING TOO STRONGLY IS A MAJOR OBSTACLE IN WISH-PRACTICE

When you use wish-practice successfully you will be able to make things happen, but that doesn't mean that you are completely in control. Quite the opposite! Wish-practice only works from a basis of humility and ultimately your desired aim can only come to you as a gift. If you have a demanding and controlling attitude based on the idea that it is *you* who makes all this happen you will be astonished how many obstacles you will encounter. Therefore, one of the most important ingredients of wish-practice is to have a light-hearted and playful attitude.

Making your wishes come true should not be a serious business. It is more like when you were a child and deeply immersed in your imaginary games. If you can pursue your aims now with the same kind of humorous and creative playfulness you are half-way there.

If you look at the first three steps of wish-practice they are more or less common sense: first, you need to know what you want; second, you need to focus on your aim; and third, you need to do something that is conducive to your aim. The fourth step is letting go of your craving and it is a little bit more difficult to understand. You can try another little exercise to find out why 'wanting too strongly' is such a major obstacle.

Exercise
Find Out Why Craving for Your Wish is an Obstacle in Wish-practice

Do this once

- Measure again on the scale from zero to ten how are you feeling at the moment.

- Focus again on your wish to be happier. Even if you are happy already, you could be much more blissful!

- Now try really hard to be happier! Try harder! Use all your will-power to force more happiness to come into your life. Do this for at least two minutes.

- Measure your well-being again on the scale. In all likelihood, and if you have really tried hard enough, you are at least one or two points *down* on the scale.

- Ask yourself why you feel worse although you were trying so hard to be happy.

The answer is probably obvious. When you use your will-power in a way that is too controlling, if you crave and want something too much, you will block the process and therefore you will not get what you desire.

The primordial ground from which our wishes arise is the most subtle level of the universe and therefore it can only be influenced by a *light and gentle* touch.

On the other hand, if our will-power is greedy and controlling it has become too crude, so it can't be used any more for the subtle process of influencing the primordial ground.

To lure things from the primordial ground into existence can be compared with luring a wild bird to eat from your hand. In both processes you need to be determined, but patient and gentle at the same time. The moment you become impatient and try to 'force' the bird it will be gone. In the same way the primordial ground will resist when it is approached with irritation and greed. It's just the way it works.

Wish-practice is all about learning to use your will-power in the right way. If your will-power is too weak and you don't really want anything, for whatever reason, you can't achieve anything. But if your will-power is too controlling and grasping you can't achieve much either. When your will and your ability to let go come together to the right degree you can achieve a lot!

WE LIVE IN A MAGICAL WORLD

When I talk to people about wish-practice many can follow me to this point. But the next question I get asked is how to make more complex or material wishes come true. People can somehow imagine that thoughts and feelings arise from space. But what about jobs, mountains and soulmates? Where do they come from? They can't possibly have just 'popped up' from space.

The answer is that everything – really everything – comes from this space. It just appears to us that mountains are completely solid and unmoveable. But even huge mountains are made of atoms and if you know your quantum physics then you know as well that an atom is, at its deepest level, nothing but space and energy. This means that physical objects are simultaneously real and solid, while at the same time being empty and non-existent. In other words, the mountain, like anything else in the physical world, is born in every moment from the primordial space. People who are very advanced in wish-practice can use this insight to walk through walls or to materialise physical things.

But don't worry, you don't need to be able to materialise

things before you can have the four-wheel drive vehicle you wish for. If you do wish-practice in order to get a car there are a thousand ways for it to come to you. Maybe you get a pay-rise and you can just buy it, or perhaps your cousin wins in the lottery and gives you his old car as a present. No matter how your desired thing finds its way to you, the basic assumption is that reality is not as solid and fragmented as we usually assume.

If you can see this fascinating magic that makes up the world and use it for your benevolent wishes wonderful miracles are possible.

However, I know that it is hard to see the magic when you are travelling on the tube on a Monday morning, when you think of the 300 unsuccessful job applications you have made, and when you have been single for years.

When I was in my early twenties I was really unhappy. I mean really unhappy, not just a bit down and confused. Life felt like hell. If somebody had read out the above lines to me I would have laughed if I hadn't been so depressed and cynical. But it was 'seeing this magic' and believing that a happy life is possible that enabled me and my whole life to change.

DOING YOUR BIT AS WELL

By successfully influencing the primordial space you are definitely working magic, but this is only half of the equation – you have to do your bit as well in order to make your wishes come true. First of all, it is not enough to sit snugly on your sofa, making powerful declarations and sharpening the tool of your concentration. Even if you can open your heart and send out a wonderful amount of love your desired aim usually doesn't come to your doorstep with a bunch of flowers in its hand. You have to go out and actively search for it. You have to make telephone calls and try to get help from people who are more experienced than you are.

You have to do everything that common sense dictates to work on your dream.

Using wish-practice will help you to enhance your intuition and it will guide you to the right people, to the lucky opportunities and eventually to the situation where everything falls into place.

There is even more you have to do, and that is to align your whole way of behaving, speaking and thinking with your wish. If you want to start your own business you can't go on sleeping every day until 10 o'clock. If you want to buy a house you can't show the estate agents how much you detest them and if you want a partner you should stop complaining to potential lovers how hard done by you were by your previous partner. Instead, you have to give out what you want to get and you need to be loving and generous to everyone. If you want people to buy your products, you must provide good quality and excellent service, and if you want the help of experts, you need to show gratefulness and appreciation.

This is really common sense and most people will find it pretty obvious. However, if you look at how many of us *behave*, it is a different matter. It is easy to forget that we can only receive in the long term what we have given in the past or what we are willing to give in the future.

The next thing you have to do in order to meet your wishes half-way is to raise your own vibration. What does that mean?

As a plant can only grow in the right soil a wish can only manifest in the appropriate circumstances. The most important circumstance for wish-practice is the state of your own mind. For example, if you want to be famous but you are still full of inner guilt about having lots of attention your wish can't manifest. First you have to let go of your guilt and to raise your vibration to a point where you consider yourself absolutely worthy of your fame. If you wish to have really loving friends, but you are quite angry and depressed yourself, it will be difficult for your wish to manifest. Again, you have to raise your vibration to the level of love and friendliness in yourself before you can have the loving friends you desire. Basically, you have to learn to be as happy, content and loving in yourself as you wish to feel when your wish is fulfilled. That sounds more difficult than it is and you can learn how to do it in Step 4 of wish-practice.

CAN WISH-PRACTICE MAKE YOU OMNIPOTENT?

If you have followed me so far you might come to the conclusion that wish-practice can make you into a powerful god who can create your own universe.

Unfortunately you are only half right, because there is something that interferes with this wonderful idea, namely other people. If we were all trying to create our own version of a perfect universe things would become a bit chaotic. One person would create a world of love and light and the next person would create a barbaric scenery with himself as the chieftain. Different people would create different kinds of worlds that would mirror exactly the state of mind they were in.

In order to avoid the chaos that would ensue if we could all wildly create anything we wanted, people have come up with a genial solution.

On some deep level we have all unconsciously agreed to believe in some basic assumptions about how our universe works.

For example, I think it's fair to say that we all believe we live in a world that follows the physical laws. That means we assume that mountains are solid and unmoveable, so we

hurt our toes if we stub them against a rock. When somebody mentions the colour blue we know what that means
and we all know that we can't fly like birds. These shared
beliefs make it possible for us to move around in a world that
we all perceive more or less in the same way, at least on the
physical level. These mutual basic assumptions about our
physical reality are difficult to change.

But Buddhist teachers tell us that this so-called objective
reality is actually nothing else but our mutual belief system.
The apparently solid world in which we live is made by our
mutual intention. That's a mind-boggling concept, isn't it?

An interesting experiment, which was done by serious
scientists, seems to prove exactly what the teachers have said.
The scientists programmed a computer to produce a
random pattern of black and white dots on a huge computer
screen. There was a large audience of people looking at this
screen and these people were asked to visualise a black ball
appearing on the screen. To the amazement of everybody,
the computer that was programmed to produce just random
patterns created a clearly visible black ball in the middle of
its screen. These people had influenced a physical thing like
a computer merely with their intention.

I wonder if doing this experiment changed the belief
system of the people who participated in it or if they all went
home believing as strongly in their physical universe as
before. It is very difficult to crack our deep-seated assumptions about the physical universe.

Even if we hear about people who can do extraordinary
things with their bodies, like sticking big pieces of metal
through their cheeks or other things that make us shudder,
we just think about it as a curiosity. And when we hear reports
about people like Uri Geller who can bend spoons we don't
really understand that these people are not outside the order
of the universe but actually demonstrate the *real* order of
the universe. We don't understand that *we* can influence the
world with our will-power. Everybody can do it.

Still, to influence our physical reality in a very direct way is difficult because we have these deep-seated shared beliefs about it. But we probably have all experienced that we each live in quite different personal and psychological worlds.

How often did you talk about an event you shared with somebody only to find out that you perceived the situation in a completely different way to the person you talked to? How often did you argue with your spouse about something that he has just said and which he now, only one minute later, vigorously denies? It is said that judges really dislike cases with many witnesses because even two witnesses never see the same version of the situation.

When I was a drugs counsellor I worked with people who lived in a kind of hell. There were women who were continuously subjected to physical violence, who were raped frequently and whose bodies and minds wasted away under the influence of alcohol, tranquillisers and drugs. I really wanted to help them but often there was not much I could do. In many cases these women just chose to stay in their hell. If they had decided otherwise the state would have provided them with a hospital bed in which to get clean, with many months of therapy in a respectful atmosphere, and with safe, supportive living accommodation. All they would have needed to do was to wish to get better. But if *they* didn't want to escape their hell there wasn't much I could do for them. My point is this:

When we do wish-practice we can create our own universe for ourselves but we can't change other people because they are creating their own personal universe.

Even if we could succeed in creating a wonderful world of love and light, we would still be aware that other people live in misery, and we couldn't take them into our world as long as they hadn't changed their beliefs accordingly. We couldn't 'make' them see that their suffering was unnecessary and that they could be much happier if they joined us or created a happier world for themselves.

The only thing we can do is to wish others well, to talk about all the possibilities that are there for everybody and to offer people help to realise them. We can invite others to join our world but we can't force them. However, the more we genuinely wish other people well the easier we make it for them to change for the better.

These are probably obvious insights to many people but it is important to point out that wish-practice has limitations. You can't make your husband talk more with wish-practice and you can't stop your wife endlessly chattering, because wish-practice doesn't give you control over other people.

GETTING HELP FROM YOUR HIGHER CONSCIOUSNESS

Wish-practice is a personal power every human being possesses and we can achieve amazing results by using it. We can become so good at it that we develop supernatural powers of all kinds and become exceedingly rich. All you have to do is practise, practise and practise for many lifetimes and completely transcend your own ego. Oh, sorry, I forgot that you wanted results in *this* lifetime!

OK, there is a short-cut to being really good at wish-practice and that is to ask for help from your Higher Consciousness. It doesn't really matter if you call your Higher Consciousness God, Divine Angels or Enlightened Buddhas. These divine beings are in essence the same as us and ultimately we are one with them. But in contrast to us humans they have never separated themselves from the primordial ground from which everything arises. They are literally one with the loving and wise qualities of the primordial ground and express them in everything they do or say.

If your wishes are based on an altruistic motivation you will come closer to your Higher Consciousness and your wish-practice will run more smoothly.

Our Higher Consciousness can only help those people who ask for its help and who are trying to live its truth. You don't even have to be a religious person to get this help. What counts is that you develop a loving heart and that you trust that there is support for you that goes beyond what you can see with your human eyes.

However, it is not enough to just ask for this help. If God or the Buddhas could make our wishes come true they probably would do that a lot more than they appear to. They certainly wouldn't stand by and watch people slaughtering each other in wars while ignoring the prayers of those who ask for peace.

Your Higher Consciousness can't significantly interfere in what is happening on this planet because if it could we would live in a happier world. All beings have free will and if they use it to make themselves and others unhappy there is nothing God or anybody else can do for them. But everybody can use their will to align themselves more with the divine spirit and, as they do so, they can transform their own life and the lives of the people who are open to their help.

In that way wish-practice will be a mutual effort between ourselves and our Higher Consciousness. Although we have to do all we can to make our wishes come true we often need the help and the blessing of the higher beings as well to bring these wishes into existence. In many cases there is an act of grace involved when we finally receive the fulfilment of our wish and therefore we have to approach wish-practice with an attitude of humility.

But equally we need confidence in our own abilities, because wish-practice is much more powerful than simply praying. If praying on its own were enough every devout person would have everything they wanted in life and we probably all know that it isn't that simple. In wish-practice we combine our personal power of influencing the primordial space with the blessing and support of the Buddha or of God. And the more we can strengthen our connection to our Higher Consciousness through prayer and meditation, the more this help will be available to us when we need it.

WISH-PRACTICE AND THE LAW OF KARMA

The law of karma is an Eastern concept and it tells us that we get back what we have done to others and that we have to give out what we want to receive in order to fulfil our wishes. This includes the idea that we have lived many lives in which we did good and bad things. Imagine that you have made some teeny-weeny negative wishes for others in this life or in previous lives. I know, it is extremely unlikely that you should ever have done something like that. But, if you did, could it be possible that some of the 'unfairness' you have experienced in your life has happened because this negativity came back to you?

OK, so you have never harmed a fly and you want me to stop suggesting things like that. But what about the wishes you had for yourself? Wishes have a strong tendency to come true, and when your desires were unconscious or on the basis of negative beliefs, the results can make you quite miserable.

Let me give you an example. When I was in my already mentioned unhappy twenties I had the strong belief that 'I would never get what I needed'. I would go around to my friends and talk and complain as if this was an unshakeable reality. Having said that, I didn't have real friends then, only some comrades in suffering. I didn't exactly wish to suffer, but because I had this negative belief that 'I would never get what I needed', it didn't seem to be a possibility to wish for something good for me, something that *would* satisfy my needs. And sure enough, all I experienced were confirmations that life was like an empty desert that left me starving and destitute. I suffered but I put up with it because it was a confirmation of what I believed was realistic.

These confirmations of our view of reality are a vicious circle because in one way or another we are addicted to them. It is as if there is a little tape on a loop behind our forehead that is constantly saying 'See, I am right. See, I am right. See, I am right.' Even if we are 'right' about negative and stupid views like 'I will never get what I need', at least we derive some satisfaction about the fact that 'I *knew* I was right'.

Then one day I read Shakti Gavain's pioneering book *Creative Visualisation* and I was hooked on this idea immediately. From that day on I visualised a happier life; I wrote affirmations into my diary and wished with all my might to have a better life. But nothing changed and I remained very unhappy. Why was that?

The answer is that wish-practice mostly doesn't work instantaneously (although it sometimes can). At that time I was still subjected to the outcome of my negative beliefs and wishes, which I had had for many years, and my newly sprouting wish-practice couldn't change the results of these negative wishes immediately.

We are all without exception in the same situation as I was then. Our lives now are the direct outcome of what we have wished for and done on the basis of our limited beliefs of the past. We might have thought it was 'normal' to experience the amount of suffering we did and that we didn't deserve any better. Real happiness, we thought, is something that only other people experience.

But here comes the good news! Not long after I started wish-practice my life started to change and over time it did so thoroughly. I also started to behave in a way that was in harmony with what I wanted and for quite a while now I have been able to say, 'I do get everything I need in abundance.'

This sounds like a 'she lived happily ever after' ending. Unfortunately this isn't quite true, because 'happily ever after' really only applies to fairy tales. Nothing lasts for ever and anybody's life can take a turn for the worse at any time when old negative karma ripens, which means that something negative they have done in the past comes to fruition. This is as true for me as it is for everybody else. We and our families can be afflicted by terrible diseases, for example, or the country in which we live can become involved in a war.

The Law of Karma and Illness

Karma is also the reason why even the finest treatments for illnesses don't work for everybody. At their best, success rates for treatment are only at 80 or 90 per cent and some people remain ill, no matter how hard they try to get better.

Buddhist teachers tell us that illnesses can have four causes: environmental influences (like living near to a nuclear power station or eating the wrong kind of food); karma (which means the illness is the result of something negative we have done in a past life); and psychosomatic reasons (these are wrong attitudes and suppressed emotions that can lead to energy blocks and illness). The fourth reason for getting ill is to take on negative karma for others out of compassion.

This last reason might explain why so many highly realised beings, who have achieved more love and wisdom than most of us, are constantly ill. But nobody can tell for sure why we are sick. Wish-practice can help us to create a radiantly healthy body, but we need to be aware that we are not completely in control because of the 'karma factor'.

I can summarise by saying that our wishes and our karma are completely interwoven. On an absolute level we can create from the primordial space whatever we want. But on a relative level we have to deal with our present world, which we have created with our past wishes and beliefs, and we have to obey its rule of karma. But even though we are subject to the outcome of our deeds of the past, we always have the freedom and the possibility to create a new and better life with the power of our wishes. According to the Buddhist teachers we don't experience the results of our karma all the time. There is plenty of space in which our new wishes can manifest if we use the opportunity. Our life is bound to improve if we use wish-practice wisely and consistently.

Some people get really upset when they hear about karma. 'Would you tell people who are ill and traumatised that it is their own fault, their own karma?' they ask. They assume that believing in karma means to stop being compassionate and to stop helping others. Nothing could be further from the truth!

No matter how bad our own karma or the karma of other people we should always try to help and improve the situation.

No bad karma lasts for ever. Once it has purified the negativity of the past our good wishes can manifest.

I find the concept of karma very comforting and relaxing. If I have lived many millions of lives as the Buddhist teachers tell us, surely I have done one or two naughty things. With this idea in mind I find it much easier to bear when people, bacteria and viruses attack me. Annoying as these attacks might be they are actually serving me well because they are *purifying* my bad deeds from the past. They redeem what I have done once and for all, and afterwards I am free from the causes I have sown many lifetimes ago, and my positive wishes can manifest.

But some people find it a big lump to swallow that we have created our life according to our own wishes. 'I didn't wish for the misery in my marriage,' they say. 'And I didn't wish for my unhappy childhood.'

Let's start with the misery in marriage. Nobody wishes to be unhappy. We all are very much alike in that we all want to be happy. The trouble is that we don't always know what brings happiness. So, we marry someone and hope secretly that they will change once we have children and become miraculously the person of our dreams. When it turns out to be the opposite we are very disappointed. Or we ignore the fact that our partner was never 100 per cent honest. When it turns out that he has had a secret lover we are shocked.

So, what happens is that we wish for happiness but we don't rigorously act on this wish. We make bad compromises and we are not aware of the warning signs. We enter into a relationship and think we have found the partner of our dreams, and a few years afterwards we feel terribly disappointed.

The Way We Choose Our Parents

Buddhist teachers have explained that we are shown different couples who could be our parents before we take rebirth and that we choose those to whom we feel drawn. This choice is made as wisely or as blindly as we would choose a spouse and, like marriage, it can be bliss or a real disaster. It is not true that our higher self lovingly chooses parents for us so that we can learn the lessons we need to learn. What kind of 'love' is it that would choose abusive parents for powerless and helpless children?

If it were true that our parents were chosen for us by a higher power in order to make us into better people this higher power would choose *model parents* for us, parents who would be as loving, happy, firm and spiritual as is desirable, because the quickest and most effective way to learn is through models that epitomise the learning goal. When people who had a horrible childhood learn and develop well it is *despite* their suffering and not because of it.

So, if you had a hard and unhappy life you need to learn to make better choices to improve your future, and wish-practice will show you exactly how to do that.

HOW DOES WISH-PRACTICE WORK, AFTER ALL?

Wish-practice is 50 per cent magic, 80 per cent your own doing, 85 per cent the help of the Higher Consciousness and 95 per cent patience. Why these numbers don't add up to 100 per cent I don't quite understand, because in terms of subjective experience they make total sense. Maybe that is because wish-practice in itself is a mystery.

The way things and beings arise from the primordial ground remains wonderfully unexplainable. Buddhist teachers say things evolve from this space like beautiful rainbows and that it is heart-stoppingly beautiful to watch this. On the deepest level the space that is the core of our being never stops being a wonderful mystery. All we can do is to be witness of its fantastic qualities and to use them in order to find love and happiness for ourselves and for others.

HOW DOES WISH-PRACTICE WORK? THE ESSENTIALS

- What we experience as our personal and psychological reality is not more real than our dreams and what we experience as our physical reality is nothing else than a mutual belief system, which we share with the people of our culture.

- Our dreamlike reality arises from the primordial ground that gives birth to everything in the whole universe. The primordial ground is boundless space, which has a living and a loving quality.

- We can influence what arises from this primordial ground through concentration, love and sound.

- Wanting too strongly and trying to control this process are major obstacles in wish-practice.

- You still need to work for the fulfilment of your wishes as common sense dictates, but the use of wish-practice will make sure that your efforts will be crowned with success.

- You can create a wonderful world for yourself, but wish-practice can't change other people against their will.

- Wish-practice is much more powerful than prayer. However, the process will go more smoothly if you can ask your Higher Consciousness for help and if you align yourself with it by making your wishes with an altruistic motivation.

- On an absolute level you can create whatever you want from the primordial ground, but on a relative level you live in an already existing world that is ruled by the law of karma. This means that everything you experience now is the result of your own past wishes and deeds, and that you have to give out what you want to have in order to create a better future.

Step 1

Finding Your Heart-wish

There are three basic truths in wish-practice and the first states, 'You can't be without wishes'.

Wishes are at the root of everything and we wouldn't even exist without the intention to do so. Without the wish to live we wouldn't eat and drink and we wouldn't go out and earn the money we need. Living means to have wishes. Even if we walk on a spiritual path of detachment and renunciation we will still be full of wishes because to be an ascetic is just another wish. (And by the way, you need to have a lot of will-power to live as a monk or nun.)

What are your wishes at the moment? If you are aware of them you will discover abundance. I, for example, want to sit here and write an inspiring book, a book that people will like and be able to use. I wish my back would hurt less and I wish I could sit more upright as my physiotherapist has advised me to. Now I wish to take a sip from my glass. I wish that my husband will have a good day at work, that our holiday will be fun, that our son will be healthy and develop well, that I can meet my friends tonight as planned ... etc., etc.

Hopefully the above didn't bore you, but do you get my point? Our life numbers a huge amount of wishes, from wanting to go to the toilet to wanting to be enlightened. It is impossible to be without wishes, but you might be unaware of them. Even if you feel that you are drifting through life without any bigger intentions, on a deep and possibly unconscious level you probably have dozens if not hundreds of unrecognised desires.

The second truth of wish-practice states, 'You will get what you wish for.'

The primordial ground *must* give you what you concentrate on because this is how it is designed. Therefore it is a good idea to choose your desires as consciously and wisely as you can.

Are you aware of what you want in life? Do you know what you desire not only for your near future but also for your distant future and even for your future lives? Do you consciously choose your goals for *any* area of your life?

Not knowing what you want or, even worse, not allowing yourself to have wishes is limiting and can lead to a lot of unhappiness. In these areas you will probably experience what you were told by authorities in your life or what everybody else experiences around you. In the best case this will lead to a mediocre life; in the worst case you will be very unhappy because you act on the basis of wrong and limiting beliefs that you have learned from confused people.

Many of these limiting beliefs are judgements that were given to us when we were young and that we never dared to contradict: 'You are stupid!'; 'You won't find a man the way you are!'; 'You will never amount to anything!' etc., etc. If you don't consciously decide what you want in *any* area of your life, you are very likely still to obey a host of negative and limiting ideas, which come either from your personal surroundings or from the influence of the entire culture you live in.

The best way to overcome these limitations is not to fight against them but calmly to decide that you want something else. Every one of us has the ability to become extraordinarily happy and successful, no matter what our background and past.

Let me give you an example from my life. About ten years ago I opened a book in a bookshop that described the aura of people and how much more you can help your clients when you are able to see their energy fields. I was absolutely fascinated and as soon as I left the bookshop I made a fervent wish to become psychic and to see auras. However, nothing in my life encouraged me to believe that I could develop supernatural abilities.

I had never had invisible childhood friends, I had never had spontaneous recollections of previous lives and I didn't even know who was on the phone when it rang – ever. Even worse, although I knew many people who were interested in spiritual development I didn't have a clue where I could find a teacher of psychic development. Germany, where I lived at the time, had no tradition in training people to be psychic and it seemed that the last teacher of clairvoyance had died a terrible death many hundreds of years ago during a witch-hunt. In the German culture you either had to have the luck to be born with a psychic gift or you were doomed to stay blind. *Learning* to be clairvoyant was not an option. But that was exactly what I wanted.

Now, somebody who doesn't believe in wish-practice would not even have started to have an 'unrealistic' wish like this and, even if they had, they would probably have given it up if they hadn't got anywhere after some time. But one of the most important ingredients of wish-practice is never to give up on your wishes. Often the fulfilment is nearer than you think, as my story demonstrates! Five years after I had first made my wish to be able to see auras I moved to England and, lo and behold, the country was full of teachers of psychic development. I found a well-known college for psychic studies in London, where I registered at once and started my first course a few weeks later.

I was pretty nervous when I arrived and found myself in

a room with twelve strangers. Our teacher didn't lose much time with a lot of explanations but paired us up at once. She gave us some simple guidelines and then told us to close our eyes and to sense the aura of the complete stranger in front of us. I didn't have a clue how to do it. But our teacher told us that we should just say anything that came into our minds and not worry about whether it was right or wrong. So I did. Although I couldn't even see the person in front of me I told her where she was working, the problems she was encountering at work, what her talents were and what her weaknesses were.

I carried on to tell her what her childhood was like, what her major emotional challenge was at the moment and how she could overcome it. Then I waited anxiously for her feedback – I had been spot on with every point! I found it hard to believe but the course at the psychic college proved that I had been psychic all along. My only 'problem' was that I hadn't had an opportunity to find out about my abilities. Since then I have developed my psychic abilities even further with the help of other teachers. I still don't have a clue who is on the phone when it rings but I know better than ever how to help my clients and myself to achieve the life we wish for.

If I hadn't made my wish, if I had just adapted to what was 'normal' in my culture, I would never have arrived at this point. If you want to achieve extraordinary success and happiness you need to go beyond what ordinary people tell you. You must decide what *you* want in *every* area of your life, be patient and never give up on your wishes. This is the only way you can get your own hands on the steering-wheel that is directing the course of your life.

Exercise
Get Your Hands on the Steering-wheel of Your Life

*Do this once

- Make a list of every area of your life and put it in order, so that the most important area is at the top and the least important area is at the bottom. Here is an example:

  1. Spiritual development
  2. Love relationships
  3. Emotional well-being
  4. Work and finances
  5. Health
  6. Other relationships
  7. Physical appearance
  8. Hobbies, travel, etc.

- For each of these areas on your list write down roughly what you want. (It would be best to do this on some scrap paper because you will probably have to change your wishes quite a bit as you follow the instructions below.)

- Also, write down a list of what you want to stop in your life (for example, no more addicts as partners or no more bouts of winter flu).

- Write down a list of the things you want for the next few months, the next few years and the distant future.

- Write down your wishes for the people around you.

When I ask people to formulate their wishes in every area of their lives I often encounter a lot of resistance. People tell me that they will only get frustrated if they become aware of all their unfulfilled desires and dreams, and they are afraid that they could fail to make them come true.

However, the evidence is that most people actually feel exactly the opposite. When they allow themselves really to dream and to formulate bold ideas they usually feel excited about it. It doesn't make them feel despondent, but on the contrary it fills them with energy and often exhilaration.

You see, you are given a wish-fulfilling jewel and you probably have never used it! Allowing yourself to dream about your wishes is like taking your wish-fulfilling gem out of its precious box for the first time, admiring its beauty and feeling the tingling joy of anticipation about what it will bring to you.

There is another reason why it is a good idea to formulate your wishes. The deep wishes we have are often like road signs that point to our best talents and in that way to our deepest happiness. If we don't allow ourselves to pursue our wishes we can never unfold our whole potential and achieve what we were intended to achieve. In other words, we will rot inside. Our talents will waste and we will have to live with the frustration of an unfulfilled life.

Frustrated and unfulfilled people are usually not greatly inspiring because they don't have much to give. But if you formulate your wishes, you can be a great inspiration for others, even if your desires are not fulfilled yet, because you have something to look forward to. You are neither cynical nor boring, so you will be very attractive. And the more attractive you are the easier your wishes will be fulfilled.

Wishing for what you want doesn't take much time. You can do it even if you are a single working parent and if you have neither the time nor the energy to do a lot to change your fate. The mere fact of wishing will set into motion a power that will finally draw together the circumstances that can liberate you from everything that is oppressing you, while keeping what is dear to your heart.

'But aren't some wishes an escape from reality?' somebody might ask.

Listen to this – there is no one reality given to all of us to which we have to adapt whether we like it or not. This so-called reality we live in is nothing other than our mutual belief-system, which is continually held up by what is told to us and by what we are telling ourselves. But we don't have to believe in this; instead we can *create* our own reality. This is not mad, but rather it is the sanest thing you can do. As a psychotherapist I am confronted day after day with people who *have chosen to believe* that life is a misery. I myself have believed this, and I can tell you that I was very good at it because I have a strong will. But then I chose to believe that life could make me and others really happy and so it did (after some time).

My job as a psychotherapist is to awaken my clients to the awareness that they can choose to live in a better reality if they want to. However, it is a hard job, because everybody clings to their view of reality for dear life. I have heard people saying that anyone who doesn't work in an employed job is escaping from reality, that everybody who doesn't go through painful emotional crises is just escaping and that everybody who doesn't believe certain things will go to hell.

For these people, 'reality' and 'being realistic' means to be working in an employed job, going through a lot of emotional pain and thinking that the only truth is what their church told them. They don't understand that they are only following their personal views and that those views are only true for them because they have chosen to believe in them.

This world, this so-called reality, is totally different for different people according to what they want to believe. For one it is a living hell and for another it is a true paradise.

Look for a moment out of your window and imagine you see a house there. If you are paranoid you will assume that terrorists are hiding in it, ready to come out to attack you. If you are depressed, you will think that the people in the house will never give you any kind of support and that the house is in a dismal and depressing state. If you feel a bit dull and uninspired you will find the house boring and staid. If you are really happy you will delight in the beauty of the house and in the niceness of the people living in it. And if you are very advanced on the spiritual path this house will appear to you like a beautiful palace and your heart will flow over with love and compassion for the people who live inside. Can you see, it is all in your mind!

What do *you* perceive when you look out of your window? Do you realise that you could see the same scenery in a much more inspiring way as well as in a much more depressing way? Do you realise that you could perceive the entire world in a much more blissful way without being any less 'realistic'?

If you want to experience your life as delightful and truly fulfilling the first and most important step is to wish for it – deeply and whole-heartedly.

CHOOSE WISHES THAT WILL MAKE YOU TRULY HAPPY

If you took a three-year-old girl into a huge toy shop and told her that she could choose three toys, what do you think would happen? Do you think she would wander around for a long time in order to make a wise and considerate choice? That is not very likely. It is much more probable that she would grab greedily for the first three things that looked enticing to her.

I don't want to sound like a strict nanny but I am afraid that most adults behave like greedy toddlers when it comes to wishes. 'There is another boy with an ice-cream – I want one too!' says the child. The adult says 'All my colleagues live in detached houses – I want one too!' or 'All the other women have a cleaning lady – I want one too!'

However, if you do get your cleaning lady, all the other women will already have a second car, a gardener or something else equally desirable. So you will want all that as well, only to find that once you have got it you will be dissatisfied again because the other women will have yet more things that you don't have. Wishes that are born from comparison, competition and envy will *never, ever* make you happy. On the contrary, wishes like this will put you on a relentless treadmill of greed and frustration. In order to escape this treadmill you need to find and pursue only those wishes that are road signs to happiness.

Almost all wishes can make you genuinely happy if they contain one certain ingredient. *Without* this ingredient, pursuing your wish will put you straight back on the treadmill of greed and frustration, but *with* this ingredient, your wish, whatever it is, will have the ability to turn your world gradually into a paradise. What is this ingredient?

If you want your wish to make you truly happy you need to combine it with altruistic love.

This is the third truth of wish-practice and it states, 'Only wishes that include altruistic love can make you happy.' This means that you need to have the motivation to contribute to the well-being of *others* through the pursuit of your *own* wishes in order to find the happiness that you desire.

If members of the unlucky White family who owned the monkey's paw had known about this simple truth they could have spared themselves a lot of misery. If they had added to their wish for money 'for the best of all beings', they could have used their wish-fulfilling gem to create happiness instead of disaster.

Luckily, not all our wishes end in tragedies like the Whites had to endure. But if people don't have an altruistic motivation with their personal wishes they can never find true satisfaction. Here's another example. Imagine you want to be a world-renowned flautist but you want it only for yourself and there is no love in your wish. Now imagine that your wish is fulfilled. You go on world tours and you play almost every evening to full houses. At first you love the applause you get and it gives you a real buzz. But after a few months of success you are getting used to all the appreciation and it will fail to make you very excited any more. There is no love in your heart, and at night when you go to your dark and empty hotel room you wonder why being a world-famous flautist leaves you disillusioned and depressed.

How different it would be if you add to your wish of being a world-renowned flautist the wish that you want to use your music to make other people deeply happy. You want to touch their hearts and awaken a dimension in them that can only be called spiritual. When you play your music your heart flows over with love. When you hear the applause you like it, but more important is your gratitude that you have succeeded in making people deeply happy. When you go home to your dark and empty hotel room you still carry this happiness and love in your heart, and you feel like the happiest person in the world.

Can you see the difference? If your wish doesn't contain love and happiness for other people it will soon leave you dissatisfied. The more you do what you really want to do *and* the more your wish benefits potentially all beings, the more it will make you and everybody else happy. For those of you who liked maths at school I can illustrate this point in a diagram. (For those of you who hated maths, it is still worth a look.)

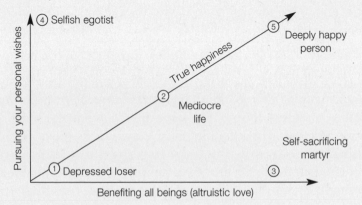

This diagram illustrates the following points:

- You will be most unhappy if you don't allow yourself to pursue any of your wishes and if you don't want to make a contribution to others either. This position (1) is one of a severely depressed person.

- If you pursue some wishes to a small degree, and you have limited love for a few people around you, you will get what most people have – (2) a mediocre life.

- If you think only about others and don't allow yourself to pursue your own ideas you can't be very happy either. You might be thinking that you are doing the morally right thing but you will feel tired and, after some time, bitter as well. You will be (3) a self-sacrificing martyr. An example would be a depressed and guilt-ridden mother who'd rather pursue a career but who doesn't allow herself this wish or isn't even aware of it.

- If you think only about yourself and you have no wish to benefit others you might get a short-lived buzz from your achievements but no deep fulfilment. Everybody knows at least one Mr or Mrs Selfish who would fall into this category of selfish egotist (4). If these people were genuinely happy their happiness would be infectious and you wouldn't feel so uncomfortable in their presence.

- The only chance for deep happiness and fulfilment (5) is if you pursue your own personal wishes with all your energy, while at the same time wanting to benefit potentially all beings.

Some people think that pursuing their own wishes and being full of altruistic love at the same time is an irreconcilable contradiction. However, in most cases there are ways of using your own wishes in order to add value to the lives of others. Let me give you some examples of how people have brought these two different attitudes together beautifully.

Pursuing your personal wish	and	having an altruistic attitude at the same time
Wanting to build up your own business	and	Wanting to create excellent quality and service for your customers; wanting to earn good money for your family; wanting to create well-paid and satisfying jobs for your employees, etc.
Wanting to have a swimming pool in your garden	and	Wanting to bring a great joy to your kids; wanting to share it with a lot of other people, etc.
Wanting to have a partner	and	Wanting to make your partner happy; using the love and happiness that is created in your relationship to benefit other people, etc.
Wanting to be happy in yourself	and	Wanting to pass this happiness on to others.

It is not 'bad' or 'wrong' to make wishes without altruistic love, it's just not very efficient – it will not bring you happiness. It can't, because the core of happiness is love and without love there will be no happiness. It is as simple as that.

However, it will not be enough if you want to benefit just a few people around you, like your family and your close friends. True altruistic love means that you want to benefit potentially *all* beings with your wish. Even if you don't reach all of them (which is of course not very likely) you need to have the attitude to not exclude anybody from your good intentions.

But here is one word of caution. Don't get altruistic love mixed up with an attitude of over-protecting, over-caring and spoiling other people. Altruistic love does *not* mean doing things for others that they could (and should) do for themselves. In fact, doing this is the opposite of love because it makes people dependent on you and in that way you hamper them instead of helping them. Altruistic love needs some wisdom as well, which means responding to the genuine needs of people rather than to their superficial demands. For example, it means you teaching your friend to get out of her co-dependency rather than just helping her to cope with her bad marriage and pitying her. It means you giving your money to a charity that cares for homeless people, rather than giving it to one homeless person who would probably just spend it on his next drink.

You might now be silently grumbling that all this altruistic love talk is pretty demanding and that it looks like too much work. But think for a moment. How often in life have you really wanted something, but when you got it you found that it didn't bring you the happiness you expected?

Before I understood about wish-practice these kinds of disappointments happened to me quite a few times. I wanted to be the friend of a certain woman, but once we were close I discovered that she could be really horrible. I wanted to have a certain job, but once I got it it turned out to be the most awful job I had ever had.

Even more often I found that my wishes made me happy for a while once they were fulfilled, but that my happiness wore off relatively soon once I got used to my newly achieved aim. After even more time I felt mainly fear about losing what I had acquired instead of the initial joy. A typical example was when I earned my first money. In the beginning I was absolutely thrilled, although it was only a small amount. But as time went on I got used to earning the money and after that the predominant feeling about my earnings was the misery that it wasn't enough.

However, since I now try sincerely to combine my wishes with an altruistic intention for others these kinds of frustrations just don't seem to happen any more. (Touch wood!)

Exercise
Understand the Benefit of Altruistic Love

*Do this once

- Think about a fervent wish that you had when you were young, which was fulfilled. You can even think about your first teddy bear if nothing more recent comes to mind.

- Try to remember:
  1. For how long did you feel completely thrilled about the fulfilment of your wish?
  2. For how long did you feel just happy about the fulfilment of your wish?
  3. For how long did you feel neutral about the fulfilment of your wish?
  4. How long did it take until you didn't appreciate what you had received any more and wanted something new instead?

- If you are still happy about the fulfilment of this wish you are either still in the buzz-phase (which will wear off soon, sorry to say), or your wish had been combined with altruistic love for others (congratulations, you are on the right path!).

Wanting to be happy without having a loving attitude is like taking drugs. At first you need only a small amount of the drug to get high but later on you need more and more. Even if you then take a lot of drugs you won't get a buzz any more and you just want to avoid the withdrawal symptoms. The Buddha says that we all, without exception, are doomed to have the same experience as an addict if we don't develop altruistic love. Nothing can make us happy for long if it isn't benefiting others. But having an altruistic attitude is like having a guarantee that your wish will make you happy once it is fulfilled.

There are a lot more benefits to combining your wish with altruistic love. Having an altruistic motivation will help you to feel on a very deep level that you deserve what you want, and this will keep you happy and trusting in the process of wish-practice even if your wish isn't fulfilled yet. It is the nature of love that it makes you feel good and deserving.

Even more important, wishes that are made with an altruistic attitude come true much faster than wishes that are just for yourself. I believe that this happens because the divine beings can link with us better if we are more connected with our hearts. I have observed time and time again that if you think of others and include them in your own wishes, you will experience the most unbelievable coincidences and often your wishes will be fulfilled quickly and almost effortlessly.

Another advantage of altruistic love is that people won't envy you so much once your wish is fulfilled. Because they feel that they are invited to participate in your success, their feelings of jealousy will often be replaced by rejoicing.

I hope by now I have convinced you how important it is to develop altruistic love in general and in wish-practice in particular. Now you can tackle one of the most important exercises in the whole book.

Exercise
Combining Your Wishes with Altruistic Love

Do this once

• Take your list of wishes from the exercise on page 36 and add to each of them an altruistic wish to benefit potentially all beings. (For example, 'I want to be a journalist in order to uncover unfairness and betrayal and to bring interesting and engaging news to a lot of people.')

* Also, combine the things you want to stop with an attitude of altruistic love. (For example, 'I want to stop having relationships with an unloving partner and give my love to a partner who loves me equally, so that our mutual happiness can benefit many beings.')

ASK YOUR HIGHER CONSCIOUSNESS FOR GUIDANCE

Maybe you are wondering why I am putting so much emphasis on how to find your wishes. Maybe you already know what you want and all you need from this book is for me to tell you how to achieve it. However, I need to stress how important it is that you pursue only wishes that really will make you happy. Wish-practice is a powerful tool and if your wish goes off even very slightly in the wrong direction the results could make you quite miserable.

For many people it isn't so easy to get in touch with their deep wishes, and one of the best ways to find them is to directly ask your Higher Consciousness to show them to you. As we saw in the Introduction, our Higher Consciousness is the part of yourself that is completely loving and wise, and has all the answers to your questions. At the same time your Higher Consciousness is outside yourself; it is the expression of the primordial ground and you share it with all other beings. Your personal Higher Consciousness is the Higher Consciousness of the whole universe.

In the following exercise you can learn how to get in touch with your Higher Consciousness and to experience the fulfilment of your deepest wishes. For most of the time I have been working with wish-practice I have used nothing but this exercise and it has produced miracles for me. I have taught it to hundreds of people.

Exercise
The World of Happiness

*Do this once, and then as often as you like

- Put on a piece of soft and romantic music. As you enjoy the beautiful music relax more and more. Let yourself go with every out breath and relax your whole being.

- You are now ready to meet your Higher Consciousness. You can see your Higher Consciousness as a shimmering light that has a living and loving quality, or as a beautiful angelic being surrounded by radiant light.

- See or feel your Higher Consciousness coming towards you. You can feel how your own self becomes more loving and joyful when you are touched by the beautiful presence of your Higher Consciousness ...

- Now ask your Higher Consciousness to guide you to find your deepest heart-wish, the wish that will truly bring the happiness and satisfaction for yourself and others that you desire ...

- See yourself in a village in the countryside. Look around and notice what kinds of houses and people you see and what the weather is like. Stroll through the streets until you reach the countryside. Notice the path you are walking on and the surrounding landscape. Do you see any people or animals? ...

- After a while you can see in the distance a wall stretching across the whole countryside, which is so high that you can't see what is happening on the other side of it.

- When you come nearer you see a door in the wall with a sign that says, 'The World of Happiness'. This is the entrance to deep and genuine happiness. The thought of entering the world of happiness reminds you of a time in your life when you were deeply happy and for a moment you remember that situation in every detail.

- Now you reach for the handle of the door in the wall and open the door, and as you take a step into the world of happiness you immediately feel a wonderful wave of bliss welling up inside you. This feeling is full of joy and love. And at the same time it feels deeply peaceful and serene. You can see how your body is filled with and surrounded by beautiful light.

- As you look around you can see wonderful things and beloved people and you feel even more waves of happiness surging through your whole being ...

- You can now do anything you want. You can dance, fly and meet anybody you like ... Don't limit yourself and your experience in any way. See, feel and know that your deepest wishes have come true. Everybody you encounter is as blissful and loving as you are and everybody experiences nothing except tremendous bliss ...

- Stay with these wonderful feelings and happy images for a few minutes ...

- When you are ready open your eyes and come back into the room.

Don't worry if you don't 'see' a lot when you do this exercise for the first time. What counts is what you feel. Even if you still can't formulate your wishes after doing this practice, your positive feeling will guide you in the right direction.

If, despite doing this exercise many times, you still have great difficulties in formulating your heart-wishes, look at what you find most dissatisfying in your life. Once you have pinpointed your greatest frustration, turn that into its opposite in order to formulate a wish. For example, if your greatest frustration is that you don't know what career to pursue, your heart-wish is to know what you want and to be able to put it into practice. If your greatest frustration is a feeling of dissatisfaction, which doesn't seem to have any outer cause, wish that you will be happy and satisfied, no matter what is happening in your life.

So, once again, adjust the wishes from your initial wish-list and incorporate any new ideas that came from this exercise.

MAKE YOUR WISHES PRECISE BUT NOT SPECIFIC

To get the fastest results with wish-practice it is best to be precise about what you want but not specific. What does that mean? It means that you should not wish to buy *the* beautiful house at the end of your village *next week* through *this particular* estate agent, but wish to buy *a* beautiful house *as soon as possible*, which has precisely the aspects that are important for you without defining when exactly and how exactly that should happen. If you wish for *one* particular house that should come to you in only *one* specific way it might take much much longer to get it than if you leave all these details to the primordial ground to sort out.

Don't wish to have Leonardo DiCaprio as your boyfriend but wish to find *a* man who is just like him, if this is what you want. It is not necessarily bad or wrong to stubbornly cling to your desire to want only Leonardo and nobody else. Your wish might still come true and DiCaprio might fall in love with you when he is 85 and you are his nurse in the old people's home where he lives. But this is not exactly what you had in mind when you set out to 'get' Leonardo, is it? If you limit the possibilities of making your wish come true to one single outcome, your wish might still come true, but it can take *much* longer. If you are unlucky it can even take lifetimes.

One more word of caution: you can use wish-practice to *invite* specific people into your life but you should never try to manipulate somebody with this method. It is not only impossible to force your will upon somebody in the long term, but it is also dangerous to you because your manipulation will come back negatively on you.

You can use Leonardo DiCaprio or any other man as a *model* for your wish for a soulmate, which means you can think of him when you make your wish. But you need to do this with the clear intention that he is *just* a model for your wish and that you are not trying to impose your will on him.

If you work in a job that is not satisfying you can wish that it will become more fulfilling, but it is much more effective to wish for *a* wonderful job instead, without specifying whether you mean that your old job improves or whether you will find a new and better job. In that way your wish can be fulfilled in many more ways. Your old job might transform in miraculous ways, but if that doesn't happen you might find another job that is the fulfilment of all your dreams.

The same is true for your relationships. Wish-practice can't change other people and it is a waste of time to try to improve your relationship if your partner or friend is not interested or able to take the steps that are necessary to fulfil your needs. However, if you and your partner both want to improve your relationship, wish-practice will help you to transform your existing relationship into a deeply satisfying one.

If you want to make wishes for other people you can obviously join them in their wishes if you know what they want. But if you don't know their wishes or you don't agree with them you need to be very careful. From *your* point of view it might be a good idea that your teenage son gets up every morning at six o'clock, tidies up his room immaculately and greets you with a bright and sunny 'Good morning, darling Mum!', but I am sure your son has other ideas about this. The more you want him to behave in certain ways the more likely he will be to rebel against this. The same is true for your grumpy boss, your nasty neighbour and the friend of yours who never phones you as often as you would like.

For other people you should have only one big wish: wish them true happiness!

If somebody is truly happy, he will greet you with a smile; he will not be grumpy and will have enough energy to phone you more often. No one will rebel against such a wish – on the contrary, people will love you for it! They will feel supported and loved by you and so they will become happier. And *you* will get the best friends, neighbours or bosses you could wish for.

'But what if I want one thing and my partner is against it?' you might ask.

In such a situation you need first to make sure that each of you rates your own happiness as importantly as the happiness of the other one. If this is the case you will often be able to work out a compromise that will really satisfy both of you. But if either you or your partner is selfish you need to face the fact that it will be very hard if not impossible to make your big dreams come true in such a relationship.

My husband and I are different in many respects, and strong-willed as we both are we have many opportunities to argue. But with a sincere desire to rate each other's happiness as importantly as our own we rarely have any difficulties in finding the appropriate compromises at the time, which allows both of us to pursue our dreams.

However, sometimes it can be hard to find these compromises despite the best intentions of both partners. Maybe you want another child and your partner doesn't. Maybe your partner wants to move abroad and you don't. What do you do then?

In such a case you need first to decide what is more important to you – your dream or your relationship. If you are sure that you definitely want to keep your relationship you can simply make a wish to find a way out of this dilemma that is satisfying for both of you. You can trust the primordial ground to come up with a solution that will surprise you with its ingenuity. But if your dream is the most important thing for you you can go on pursuing it and risk losing your relationship in the process. In some cases this can be the appropriate thing to do.

Here is a little test to check whether or not you have understood this point. The question is this, 'If you want to marry your boyfriend but he isn't interested, what kind of wishes can you use to improve your situation?'

Here is the answer. First you need to decide what is more important – to be married or to be with your boyfriend. If you decide you want to stay with your boyfriend even if he still doesn't want to marry you, you can wish for a solution that is satisfying for you both. But if you know that your wish to be married has priority you can wish to be happily married to *a* man and leave it open whether this man will be your current boyfriend or somebody else (possibly somebody more attractive?). Secondly, you wish that your current boyfriend will find a life that will make him truly happy, and leave it open as to whether this is a life with you or somebody else.

There are two possible outcomes of these wishes. First, you might break up with your boyfriend and go through a phase of grieving. But then you will find somebody wonderful with whom you are even happier than with your former boyfriend, and after you get married you will (hopefully) live happily ever after.

The second possibility is that your current boyfriend will sense your genuine good wishes for him and will be so touched that he will propose to you on the spot.

The moral: wish-practice can definitely bring you a really wonderful husband or wife. There are thousands if not millions of ways in which the universe can provide you with a soulmate. But if you try to use this method to force your will upon somebody you will *definitely not* get what you want.

GO BEYOND GOODY-GOODY WISHES

Goody-goody wishes are wishes that are made by goody-goody people, namely many people who consider themselves to be on a spiritual path of some kind. Believe it or not, there are not many other people who suppress their desires more than people who 'work on themselves' or who want to develop spiritually. It is very sad, but many of these men and women consider themselves to be deeply flawed and even sinful, and therefore mistrust themselves and their wishes.

Many people on the spiritual path feel extremely undeserving and there is a host of wishes that are 'forbidden' for them because they consider them to be 'selfish', 'superficial', 'self-indulgent' or even 'blasphemous'. A deeply religious woman may feel that she is not even allowed to think about a breast enlargement, and a very spiritual man might be disgusted by his secret desires for lots of money and fast cars.

Pursuing lots of wishes and living life to the full is considered by many religious people to be selfish and 'spiritually wrong'. The only wish that is allowed from their point of view is the desire to be a loving and selfless person. The way of most traditional religions is to suppress and cut out all other wishes and to focus solely on the wish to become one with the Higher Consciousness, and to live a virtuous and selfless life. The Buddha said in the second of his four noble

truths that *craving* (not wishes!) is at the root of all suffering
and many well-intended Buddhists misinterpret this teaching, using it to justify and reaffirm their own negative view
of themselves and to suppress their wishes.

However, the trouble is that this approach often doesn't
work out. The more you try to be 'good' and selfless the
more your 'lower instincts' like greed, nastiness and egotism
will surface. There are enough examples of charismatic
preachers or important persons of the Church who 'sinned'
terribly. These people are not inherently bad but they didn't
understand one important truth: that you can only advance
on the spiritual path when you do it as a 'whole' person, if
you stop trying to cut out the parts of yourself that you don't
like.

The Buddha teaches that our deepest nature is flawless
and pure, that we are basically good and wonderful beings.
That means we can trust ourselves and that we can trust our
deep heart-wishes. There is only one kind of wish you
should not allow yourself and that is the impulse to harm
yourself and others. It is really better to suppress your feelings than to take drugs or to punch your partner in the face
if you feel angry. But any suppression of other wishes will
only cause you to become tired and bitter. Instead of becoming more loving and joyful on your spiritual path you will
become more depressed and irritable.

One of my Buddhist teachers told me that people often
come to him with the concern that a certain career or life
situation might not be 'spiritual' enough. My teacher was
really bewildered by these questions because in his opinion
it didn't matter at all whether we meditate in the Himalayas
or have a successful career in business and raise a family.
The only thing that matters, he said, is whether we can bring
an altruistic motivation into our present life.

From a spiritual point of view it is not the wishes that are
the problem but the craving, the greed and the frustration
that often accompany them. (Do you remember all those

times when you wanted to bang your head against the wall because you didn't get what you wanted? That was greed.)

We are all greedy and at times frustrated if we don't get what we want. We can't help it, it's how humans are. But suppressing our wishes is not the answer. The best way to work with greed and craving is to *transform* it. Taking our greedy and impatient nature into account the Buddha has given us this wonderful method of wish-practice where we can develop spiritually *through* pursuing our own, personal and worldly wishes. As I have already explained, the way to do this is through combining your personal wishes with altruistic love for the benefit of potentially all beings.

If you work in this way every single one of your personal wishes will actually foster your spiritual development. They will make you more happy and more loving and in that way a more spiritual person who genuinely has something to give to others.

Who is more advanced on the spiritual path? A man who chuckles at his 'unspiritual' wish for wanting to buy a Porsche but who is also able to chuckle in a friendly way at the weaknesses of other people? Or a man who is condemning himself for his greed and is condemning other people as well? The answer is clear, the more love you feel and express for yourself and others the more you have developed towards your full spiritual potential.

People who 'work on themselves' often think that there is some benefit in staying in difficult situations in order to 'learn something' rather than to leave the situation and look for something better. For example, when they are unhappy in their jobs or in their relationships they don't just look for a better job or distance themselves from the person who causes them so much heartache. On the contrary, no matter how much they suffer, no matter how hopeless the situation, they stay and try to change *themselves* in order to improve the situation. Instead of demanding that their needs are met they are just trying to be less needy, and instead of rebelling against contemptuous treatment they are just trying to be detached and understanding.

I was like that. For many years of my life I just didn't know that there was an easier way to end my suffering than to stay in difficult situations and 'to work on myself'. But at some point it dawned on me that I could love and accept *myself* and change *my situation* instead. The results were overwhelmingly effective and ever since I have felt *much* happier.

There is no benefit whatsoever in staying in a destructive relationship if your partner is not interested or able to improve the situation. It is much easier to find a new partner or to be happy on your own than to try to adapt to this negative situation. In such a situation you will never be able to prosper and to unfold your whole potential. There is no benefit, either, to staying in a job where your talents and qualities are not appreciated. You can try as hard as you like to 'improve' yourself – in such a situation you will never be able to be really content.

If you are a spiritual goody-goody person (like myself) you need to be very careful that your wishes are really *your* wishes and not something you are just told to desire. 'I really wish to be less selfish so that I can go to paradise when I die' is a typical goody-goody wish. It contains painful self-improvement, it doesn't have any short-term benefits whatsoever and I am sure nobody would really look forward to it.

But in order to make your wishes come true you need as much positive emotional energy as possible because it is this energy that will make you attractive. Does your wish make you tingle with joy and anticipation all over? Do you feel positive excitement when you think of it? Is it something that *you* really want in your heart of hearts? Then you are on the right track.

BE UNREALISTIC – GO FOR YOUR HIGHEST WISH!

Some people are very cautious and when they hear about wish-practice they are willing to give it a try but only with one of their smaller wishes. They want to try out wish-practice and only if it works for them will they want to use it for their other, more important wishes as well. This is a very sensible and appropriate approach for most areas in life but for wish-practice it has one drawback – it doesn't produce impressive results.

To make smaller wishes come true you don't need to read a whole book in order to learn the magic of wish-practice. It is not very difficult anyway and if you succeed you will think that it was solely by your own doing. However, wish-practice can produce miracles and to harvest the whole benefit of this method you need to make your wish as high and as bold as possible.

This is probably a good time to explain something about the laws of attraction. I am always surprised how often one can read that like attracts like when it is so obvious that this is not true. Even children know that the *opposite* poles of a magnet are attracted to each other, not the similar ones. It is differences and opposites that create attraction in all areas of life. For example, how attracted do you feel towards buying a house or a flat just down your road, which is more or less the same as your own? Exactly, not at all, because like doesn't necessarily attract like.

How would you feel if, for the same amount of money, you could have a beautiful country mansion with a swimming pool and stunning views? Or a smart city penthouse with a roof-garden and three large reception rooms? Oh, that's another story – here comes a lot of attraction! When there are differences we have attraction, when there are similarities we have less attraction.

However, similarities are not only boring – they can create

a mild attraction because they often provide relaxation and harmony. For example, we might feel relaxed and harmonious in the circle of our *like*-minded friends, but if a stunning version of the *opposite* sex comes along the relaxation and harmony will quickly be gone and will be replaced by exciting attraction. The strongest sexual attraction will always happen between two people who are most likely opposites of each other. For example, a very masculine man will tend to fancy a very feminine woman and not a woman who has a strong masculine side like himself.

There is a third dynamic that creates attraction – we often feel powerfully drawn to what is familiar to us. This is the reason why people often end up with the same sort of partner over and over again, and why we might not endeavour to buy a new home at all and would rather stay in our familiar old shed, although it really doesn't suit our needs any more.

We feel so drawn to what is familiar to us because it provides us with a feeling of safety. No matter how awful the circumstances, no matter how limiting the relationships, familiarity provides security and that is a powerful glue. Although we might feel drawn to exciting new possibilities, to really leap beyond our old patterns can be quite scary as well. That is one of the most important reasons why so many people never go beyond what they have experienced in the past.

Here is a summary of the laws of attraction:

- The strongest attraction is caused by differences and opposites.

- We are also powerfully drawn to what is familiar to us because it provides security.

- Similarities create mild attraction because they provide harmony and relaxation.

So, if you want to use these insights for wish-practice you

need to wish for something that is really different from your current situation. You have to make a conscious choice to leave your familiar but dissatisfying patterns behind and take a courageous step into the unknown. Wish for an abundance of energy rather than for a little more energy. Don't just wish for the next promotion, wish to be the leader of a firm if this is what you want. Instead of wishing to be more loving, wish that your whole being is transformed into pure love.

Be inventive: you can create whatever you like, even if you have never experienced anything like it before. The higher your wish and the more different it is from your current situation, the more magnetic attraction it will create. This increased attraction will pull you at a much higher speed towards your desired aim, and as it does so all your smaller wishes will be fulfilled along the way. That's not too bad, is it?

There is another reason for going for your highest and boldest wishes. If you just make a small wish for the next step towards your highest goal you could easily get stuck. For example, if you wish for a boyfriend but you actually want a husband you can get in serious trouble once you have your great new boyfriend and you realise that he is not interested in marriage. It would have been much more economical to wish for a husband straight away.

'But these high wishes are not realistic!', I can hear your collective outcry.

Let me repeat, with wish-practice you are not trying to get the best from an existing reality – with wish-practice you are *creating* reality. There is no wish too high that can't be fulfilled. Think about it, just 150 years ago much of what is normal for us today would have been totally unrealistic for the people then: curing infectious diseases, flying in the air and communicating by mobile phone and over the Internet to name just a few. There are even more outrageous things to come in the near future like amazing computer technology, space tourism and stunning operations in order to save life. All these things wouldn't be possible without the passionate and fervent wishes of individuals who had only one thing in common: they had a vision and they believed in it.

But we don't need to look only at scientific achievements. There also lots of smaller and bigger 'miracles' happening around us all the time and even in our own lives. There are so many stories about people who were given only a few months to live and who recovered miraculously. Or what about people who can communicate with angels and fairies? There is an abundance of stories of astounding spiritual healing, being in two places at the same time and other miracles. Don't just dismiss these reports – some of them might really be true.

And let me ask the question again – what is reality anyway? Earlier we looked at the deep philosophical and spiritual aspects of this question, so I won't repeat them here. But let's look at what we think is 'realistic' from a more psychological and sociological point of view. When we say 'something isn't realistic', what does this mean? What kind of reference frame do we have that allows us to come to that conclusion?

Most people (or is it all?) think reality is what they perceive around them, what friends and family tell them, what scientists or priests say or what they read or see in the media.

We all think we are perceiving the correct view of reality, don't we? So, how come we all have such different opinions about what is possible and realistic? I am not talking here about your dear friends, whom you have chosen exactly for the reason that they all agree with you on your basic assumptions about what is realistic. I am talking about this colleague of yours whom you can't stand, about the homeless woman you see every day on your way to work, about someone who is seriously rich and famous and about the yogi who has meditated for the last twenty years in a cave. If you talked to all of these people about what is realistic in life you would find that they are worlds apart from what *you* think is possible. Why is that? We are all living in the same world.

The answer is that we only perceive what we *want* to perceive. In psychology this is called selective attention and it means that we *can't perceive anything other than what we believe is true*. In other words, we do not perceive reality as it is but we are constantly trying to confirm our beliefs. If, for example, a woman believes that all men are deep-down egotists, she will never, ever meet a loving man. And even if she does she will dismiss him as a bore.

Maybe all this is not new to you and you have already been familiar with these concepts for a long time. However, understanding selective attention doesn't mean you are free of it. We are all (including myself) complete prisoners of our beliefs about reality. Selective attention is the reason why so many people always end up with the same sort of partner, no matter how hard they try to change. The reason why they are repeating a familiar pattern over and over is that they *can't see* that there are better partners for them. However, there is one way out of this dilemma – *you have to think big*.

When I was a single I tried to use wish-practice to find a partner. I did what I ought to do and wrote a list about what I wished the man of my dreams should be like, which contained at least sixteen points. I also did something that I shouldn't have done and talked to my girlfriends about this list. I had a wide circle of friends then and there wasn't one of them who didn't tell me that I was being *completely* unrealistic. This kind of perfect Prince Charming, they told me, didn't exist or, if he did, he would of course have been married to somebody wonderful for decades. My friends didn't try to discourage me without reason; their own reality was proof of what they were saying. They were single themselves, divorced or lived in mediocre or difficult relationships, and they were trying to protect me from unnecessary disappointment.

However, wayward as I am I kept wishing for a man with

whom I could have the perfect relationship on *all* levels. I am proud to tell you that I have proved all my friends wrong and that I found my 'perfect' Prince Charming. Every single point on my wish-list has come true and after many years our relationship is still as blossoming and delightful as it was in our early times.

Many people are reluctant to make their wishes higher and higher because they feel they ought to know in advance how to make their desires come true. And because they have no idea how to do this they don't even dare to wish and give up before they have even started. This is a real shame because one thing is sure – without making your wish you will *never* get what you want.

You *don't need to know* right from the start how to make your wish come true because by using wish-practice you will be *guided* to your aim.

You don't need to know how to bring your spiritual aspirations together with your career in business – just wish for it! You don't need to know how at the age of sixty you could become a successful artist – just wish for it! And you don't need to know how to become blissfully happy – just wish for it! No matter what you want, if you use wish-practice correctly you will be guided to your aim in a way that you might never have thought was possible.

By having really bold wishes you can use the increased power of attraction that is created and this will pull you in the direction of your aim. In this way you will reach your goal much faster and with much less effort than you think. I have seen over and over again that practicalities sort themselves out when people have a grand vision. When you do wish-practice correctly you will find the people who will help you and the resources you need in order to make your wish come true. It is really true what the old saying tells us – 'Where there's a will there's a way'.

Remember to make the altruistic part of your wish really

big as well. If you are a healer, consultant, teacher or therapist of some kind don't imagine reaching just a few dozen clients; try to reach *millions* of them. You can wish to benefit the whole world and even future generations with your wish. And don't forget the universe. You can include all the beings on other planets in your wish as well! And what about your future lives? Even if you don't believe in reincarnation you can never be sure that you will not survive death. So it is a good idea to include all your future lives in your wishes as well.

Don't make little wishes like 'I want to have fewer arguments with my partner and a bit less stress at work.' Don't waste this great opportunity! Wish for a relationship that makes you and everybody else exceedingly happy, and to have the most fulfilling and satisfying job you can think of, which will provide excellent service for a vast amount of people in this life and all future lives together. That's a worthwhile wish using wish-practice!

So, now for the last time (I promise!) go through your initial wish-list and change your wishes to something that really makes you excited and tingling all over with anticipation. Now you can write down your wishes in a special, beautiful notebook, which you can entitle 'Book of wishes' or more boldly 'My future life'.

PRIORITISE YOUR WISHES

It is very common for people to feel torn between two or more wishes. 'Shall I move or shan't I? And if I move, shall I go south or shall I go north? Or shall I even go abroad?' The list is endless and some people are so undecided that they ruin their life with their constant doubting and ruminating.

I would even go so far as to say that most of our psychological problems are caused by unclear ideas about what we want. I can see this in myself, in my friends and family and in all my clients. If we knew exactly what we wanted and if we could pursue our aims with determination and equanimity most of our suffering would quickly dissolve. Typical conflicts are, 'Shall I stay in this relationship/job/situation and try to improve it or shall I look for another one?' or 'Shall I complain and risk a conflict or shall I try to put up with the situation?' I am sure you can add your personal conflict patterns.

Often people feel torn because they are afraid that pursuing their own wishes might harm other people. In particular parents face this conflict almost constantly. Think for example of a new mother who had lots of romantic ideas about motherhood. She might find the reality of rocking the cradle and singing lullabies excruciating, but she might feel terribly guilty as well about leaving her baby with others.

What can we do if we feel torn like this? There is another exercise that could help with these kinds of conflicts.

Exercise
Prioritise Your Wishes

Only do this when you need it

- Define clearly each of your wishes in the form of 'I want . . .'

- Arrange a chair for each wish you have.

- Sit down on the first chair and imagine that it is a year later and that your wish has been completely fulfilled. Speak out loud, and in the present tense, say how you feel about it. Stop and check how you feel. Feel your body. How relaxed are you and what is your breathing like? Do you feel weaker or stronger?

- Do the same for each of your other wishes on the other

chairs. Imagine each time that it is one year later and that your wish has been completely fulfilled. Check carefully how you feel each time.

- Check on each chair whether you envy the other versions of yourself sitting on the other chairs.

- The wish that makes you feel the happiest, the most fulfilled and the least envious has priority.

- Don't suppress your less important wishes, but try to integrate them creatively with your highest priority wish.

The last point of this exercise is very important. Let me give you some examples of how people have integrated their wishes in a way that satisfied them.

Highest priority wish	Less important wish	Integration of wishes
Staying in a job.	Becoming self-employed.	Starting some small business on the side.
Staying married.	Getting divorced.	Telling your spouse that you will get divorced if nothing changes.
Staying at home with your baby.	Going to work.	Doing some work at home and getting a babysitter who will look after the baby in the next room.

A typical sort of conflict is the question: shall I pursue my wishes or shall I be a goody-goody person who puts other people's needs first? Luckily, there is a clear answer to this problem. Only if you regard your needs to be *as* important as the needs of the other person can you find happiness for everybody involved. Whenever your own wishes seem to be in conflict with the wishes of somebody else, the solution is to find a compromise that will make *both* people happy. Most people are happy to find compromises when they see that the other person is compromising as well. In this way we are not very different from kindergarten children. They don't make a fuss if they get only one biscuit as long as everybody else gets only one too.

If we constantly put other people's needs first we might feel in a morally superior position, but that will not protect us from becoming bitter after a while. And, if we constantly put our own needs first, we would be happy if it wasn't for this little voice in the back of our mind that is constantly telling us that we are selfish. How do we silence it?

The satisfying solution is to find compromises that make *both* people happy. Not only yourself – not only the other person – but both. This is called a win-win situation and in such a conflict we don't have a loser and we don't have just one winner – we have two contented winners.

STEP 1, FINDING YOUR HEART-WISH: THE ESSENTIALS

In Step 1 you learned how to put your hands on the steering wheel that that is steering your life by making wise wishes that will definitely lead to happiness in all areas of your life.

- The three basic truths of wish-practice are:

  1. You can't be without wishes.
  2. You will get what you want.
  3. Only wishes that include altruistic love can make you happy.

- Formulate wishes for all areas of your life so that you will not be ruled by your unconscious negative beliefs and assumptions.

- Combine your personal wishes with altruistic love for potentially all beings. Think of as many ways as possible in which you could contribute to the well-being of others through the fulfilment of your own wishes.

- Ask your Higher Consciousness to show you your heart-wish.

- Make your wishes precise but not specific. (*A* house, rather than *this* specific house.)

- Don't force your will on other people and wish for them only that they will find true happiness. It is not possible to change other people with wish-practice.

- Make sure that your wishes are really *your* wishes and make you tingle with joy all over.

- Make sure that your wishes don't contain painful self-improvement and that they include some benefits for the nearer future.

- Formulate your wishes as high and bold as possible. In that way you will create a lot of attraction.

- Don't worry if you think your wish is unrealistic and if you don't know how to make it come true. By using wish-practice you will be guided to your aim.

- Prioritise your wishes if you feel torn between two or more alternatives.

Step 2

Strengthening Your Wish-power

Now it's time to get serious!

If Step 1 was taking your wonderful wish-fulfilling gem out of its precious box, Step 2 will show you how you can polish your jewel to remove any blemishes and use its power to work magic. In Step 2 you will learn how to use and to strengthen the magic tools of your heart-mind.

MAKE YOUR WISH MORE PRECISE

You can work on as many wishes at the same time as you like, but I recommend that you choose one wish on which you want to focus primarily. This wish is called your heart-wish. If you have followed Step 1 of wish-practice your heart-wish now looks like this:

- You have consulted your Higher Consciousness and you are sure that this wish comes from the depth of your being and that it is what *you* really want.

- It is the highest aim you can imagine.

- You have combined your wish with altruistic love so that its fulfilment will be of benefit for potentially all beings.

- You have formulated your wish in an unspecific way ('a job in *a* great computer company', instead of 'a job only with IBM'), because you would otherwise limit your options too much.

- Your wish is not only a long-term goal but also includes some benefit for the nearer future.

- You can stay basically as you are in order to receive your wish (no painful self-improvement required).

- You have prioritised your wishes in case you felt torn.

- You feel excited and joyful about your wish.

The next step is to make your wish even more precise. Why is this so important?

Let's imagine wish-practice is like a mail-order catalogue (in fact, it is so much like a mail-order catalogue that it is hard to believe). You wouldn't just phone the friendly salesperson and say 'Please send me a pair of trousers', would you? Even if you did and even if they did send you a pair of trousers, the likelihood is that they would be of the wrong size, style, fabric and colour. So, like you would do when you order something from a catalogue, you need to tell the primordial ground exactly what you want. The primordial ground will deliver precisely what you tell it, so don't lose time and energy by giving it vague ideas and then rejecting them afterwards.

By the way, wish-practice is even better than mail-order catalogues because it can give you much more than any catalogue can. For example, from a catalogue you can order a pair of trousers in a specific size, colour, style and so on. But you can't order clothes that will definitely suit you, flatter your figure and make you feel great about yourself. But with wish-practice you can do just that. When you 'order' your wishes you need to specify exactly how you want to feel on all levels when your wish is fulfilled.

I think it's fair to say that all people want to be deeply happy. Whatever we wish for, whatever we desire, in the end we all want one thing – we want to be genuinely happy. So, in order to find this happiness you need to be sure that your wish will make you happy, once it is fulfilled. However, although everybody wants to be happy, it can be startling to observe how many people continuously pursue aims that will bring them none of their desired happiness, but will leave them dissatisfied at best and very unhappy at worst.

Take for example the desire to be rich. It is astounding how many otherwise intelligent people still assume that lots of money will bring them lots of happiness. They don't realise that money will *only* make them genuinely happy if they use it for purposes that will contribute to the happiness of others. Only then can they find the deep fulfilment that is the motivating force behind any wish.

Altruistic love is the only source of true happiness, but we have to be very careful not to get a wrong slant on it. Some people will quickly end up becoming too self-sacrificing and others will ignore the altruistic-love bit altogether. So, to be sure that your wish will make you happy, you need to ask directly for it. The next exercise will show you what you need to be deeply happy with your wish.

Exercise
Make Your Wish More Precise

*Do this once

- Write on the top of a sheet of paper, 'In order to be really happy with [state here your wish], I need ...

- Without too much effort, allow a thought, a feeling or an image to come up and complete the sentence.

- Write down whatever comes into your mind even if it seems unrealistic or impractical.

- Repeat the beginning of this sentence at least ten times and each time write down what comes into your mind.

From here you can go directly to one of the most important exercises in wish-practice. You have to write a detailed wish-list that consists of five parts: first you have to describe exactly what you want (remember the mail-order catalogue). Secondly you have to describe how you want to benefit potentially all beings with your wish. That is the already much-discussed altruistic-love bit. In the third part you have to state precisely how you want *to feel* on all levels once your wish is fulfilled. The fourth part deals with what you want to avoid in future. If you have a long story of failures in the area of your wish (for example five times divorced and ten times sacked), you need to be very sure that you are not drawn into making the same kind of mistake all over again. In the last and fifth part of your wish you should write a short summary of the two or three most important and non-negotiable aspects of your wish.

Leave it totally open *how* your aim should be fulfilled and let the primordial ground sort out all the practicalities. Usually it is not necessary to wish for money because it is not an end in itself. Instead wish for a feeling of financial security for yourself and your family or wish directly for anything that you would like to buy. You never know, you might get your desired object as a present. Similarly, don't describe *when* your wish should be fulfilled. Your primordial ground knows that you want it as soon as possible and so it will be. However, 'as soon as possible' might be next year, even if you want it tomorrow.

Exercise
Write a Wish-list

*Do this once

1. Describe all the aspects of your wish that are important to you.

2. Describe every possible detail of how you want to benefit potentially all beings with your wish.

3. Describe how you want to feel on all levels once your wish is fulfilled (emotionally, spiritually, mentally and physically).

4. Write a list of what you want to avoid under all circumstances (for example, no more working with difficult teenagers, no more than two commitments in the local community, no more partners who can't take care of themselves).

5. Summarise your whole wish-list into the two or three most important and non-negotiable points.

The examples below show you how *not* to write your wish-list.

1. Describe all aspects of your wish

- 'I want to be a teacher and it doesn't matter what I earn and what the school is like as long as I have a job.' (You need to be *much* more precise to find a place where you would really enjoy working.)

- 'I want to work only in the school up my road.' (Too specific – it might take ages for you to find a job there.)

- 'I am open, I can work anywhere.' (In order to bring out

your special talents you need a place that is tailor-made for you. You need to have at least one or two non-negotiable aspects.)

- 'It isn't realistic to expect to enjoy working as a teacher. The best I can hope for is a bearable situation.' (Nonsense! You *can* create a wonderful life if you really put your will behind it.)

- 'I wish to be less demanding and to be happy in the difficult school I am working in at the moment.' (This is a typical goody-goody wish that will make neither you nor anybody else happy, nor will it earn you any points in the after-world. So you might as well try to wish for something that you want more deeply.)

2. Describe how you want to contribute to the world with your wish

- 'I want to teach the children so that they will have a good start in their life. But I will favour the girls because men have dominated women long enough.' (In your next life you will probably be born as a boy and encounter a teacher like yourself. So be careful what you wish for!)

- 'I can't think of anything altruistic because being a teacher is so exhausting.' (Are you sure you really want to be a teacher? You might be much happier in a totally different job.)

- 'I want to do anything for my pupils, so that they will love me.' (In this section you should *not* focus only on yourself for a change. Besides, benefiting others doesn't mean doing 'anything' for them because that would only spoil them and make them dependent on you. Benefiting others means helping them to help themselves.)

- 'I want to try really hard to be more giving and to ask less for myself.' (Stop this goody-goody nonsense at once!

Wish-practice is not about becoming more self-sacrificing but about how to become genuinely happier so that you will *really* have something to give to others.)

3. Describe how you want to feel on all levels

- 'I want to feel good.' (You need to be much more precise. You will not be satisfied if you feel good emotionally but are intellectually unfulfilled with your pupils, or the other way around.)

- 'It isn't realistic to expect to *always* be happy.' (Are you sure? Remember, with wish-practice you are *creating* reality and if you believe that you can't be continuously happy you will definitely be right!)

4. Describe what you want to avoid

- 'I don't need to avoid anything because I am such a positive and open-minded person.' (Don't be too sure. Everybody needs to make clear decisions to find a life that is really satisfying.)

- 'I want to avoid state schools and private schools, small children and teenagers.' (If your avoid-list is longer than your wish-list you might actually want something totally different. Write in this section only those things you found difficult in your past.)

Now, in order to balance all these possible mistakes, look at this wish-list of a client of mine, which was done in a very skilful way.

Wish For a Car

1. Describe all aspects of your wish

I want a safe, reliable, economical (both to buy and to run), nice-looking car. It needs to be spacious – probably an estate. Price: not more than £3,000.

2. Describe how you want to contribute to the world with your wish

My car will enable me to keep my work commitments without stress on myself (which will make me a more effective and inspiring teacher). It will also bring happiness to my children and friends by offering them reliable transport and by keeping my commitments to them.

3. Describe how you want to feel on all levels

Physically safe and comfortable; emotionally exhilarated and secure – also not self-conscious that I look a failure in financial (worldly) terms; spiritually that I am using the fulfilment of my wish to contribute to the increase of happiness of my students, children, friends and others.

4. Describe what you want to avoid

Owning an embarrassing, rotten-looking rust-bucket that drips oil on my drive, believing I only deserve the bare minimum, and worrying about the vehicle, its maintenance and how I will buy my next car after this one.

5. Summary

Reliable, economical and decent-looking car.

My client found a car that fitted all the above requirements just one week later for only half the money he had originally been willing to spend.

Number four on the wish-list (What do you want to stop?) is very important for people who have experienced the same failure in the area of their wish more than once. However, some people might not like this part of the exercise because they believe that they should think entirely positively. I don't agree. One of the most important abilities to create the life of your dreams is to say 'no' when you mean 'no' and to say 'yes' only when you have found what you really want.

We all are drawn back to our past in one way or another.

If your past was unsatisfactory and unhappy you have to learn to say 'no' each time you are offered the opportunity of repeating your same old pattern. It is amazing how often this can happen.

'No' is such an easy word – only two letters! But how difficult it is to say it! We fear we will lose the love and support of the people around us if we are not compliant enough, and we are scared to go our way alone if nobody wants to come along.

When I was single men would sometimes fall in love with me; I received love-letters from people I hardly knew and other sorts of romantic approaches. It was wonderful! However, out of all these men approaching me there wasn't a single one who didn't have some problem with alcohol or drugs then or in their past. I really don't know why but I was highly attractive to men like that.

Once I attended a self-development seminar with 150 people, half of them men. At some point I did some work on myself and when I sat down I felt a bit shaky and tearful because it had been quite scary to talk about myself in front of 150 people. So I cried a bit on the shoulder of my neighbour and he was very nice and comforting. Later, in the break, he told me that he was a cocaine addict and that he had already spent twenty years in prison for his addiction and related crimes. At first I was shocked but then I had to laugh about his revelation. How was it possible that I could have chosen, out of seventy-five available men, the one who had such a terrible addiction?

The answer to this question, of course, is that we are always drawn to the same old things again and again. In order to stop meeting any more addicts I had to say no many times although this really wasn't easy. Some of the men approaching me were very attractive and I really didn't like to be single. If I hadn't made my strong resolution to say 'no' I am sure I would have succumbed and entered another dead-end road. However, after a while this annoying dynamic stopped, and the rest of story I have already told you.

If you have any kind of destructive pattern in your life, you really need to learn to say this difficult little word 'no' and you have to say it as often as you need until the negativity stops.

In the next exercise you will explore exactly what you have to say 'no' to in order to change your life.

Exercise
Learn from Your Failures

*Do this once and only if you have had a long row of failures in the area of your wish

- Determine the area of failures you want to analyse (for example 'frequent relationship break-ups' or 'three times bust').

- Write a history of your failures. Write down each case of failure, including how things started, how they developed and how they eventually failed.

- Find out whether all these examples had something in common.

- Draw a conclusion as to what you have to change in your behaviour and to what you have to say 'no' in future.

GET YOUR WHOLE BEING BEHIND YOUR WISH

Most people think that they have only *one* personality in the same way as they have only *one* body. Nothing could be further from the truth! In each one of us there lives a multitude of subpersonalities. At first we often have the goody-goody personality who only wants to eat small quantities of raw, fat-free and salt-free food, who wants to say only nice and compassionate things, and who wants to work very hard. However, there are many more subpersonalities in us. Take, for example, the childlike personality who doesn't care about working hard and eating healthy food. All *she* wants is to have fun. Another personality that most people carry within them is this foul-mouthed being who curses under his breath and says really nasty and vicious things about perfectly nice people. There are lots more subpersonalities in each of us and if we had a body that represented all of them we would look like a monster with at least ten heads.

There is nothing wrong with this state of being. It is natural and healthy to have many subpersonalities. If we didn't have a genius in us, for example, we would never have really original ideas. What is unhealthy is to suppress those personalities in ourselves that we don't like. In this way we create an inner war, which leads to a lot of tension and stress.

Somebody who is healthy and mature has learnt to live in peace with all their inner subpersonalities and makes decisions on which all their subpersonalities can agree. Let me put it this way: your inner psyche is like living in a house with lots of people and although they all have very different characters and opinions you can't throw anybody out. You have only one choice – either you make peace with all your subpersonalities or you live in constant war with each other.

What does all this mean for wish-practice? It means that you need all your inner subpersonalities to agree on your wish. Then you get the power of your whole being behind your aim instead of losing time and energy by endless fights within yourself. For example, *you* might wish for a passionate sex-life but your inner nun finds it inappropriate for a woman to moan and groan with pleasure. *You* might want a stunning career but your inner left-wing student finds people who make a lot of money despicable. *You* want to build up your own business but your inner lazybones just wants to chill out in front of the television.

If you have these kinds of unresolved inner quarrels you will not get very far in wish-practice because it is like trying to drive your car while pressing on the brake at the same time.

In the following two exercises you will find out what you can do to align all your subpersonalities to your wish. Even if you assume that they have all already agreed on your wish you should do at least the first of these exercises to rule out the possibility that any half-conscious negative belief is sabotaging your dream and preventing it from coming true.

Exercise
Find Out Your Beliefs About Your Wish

*Do this once

- Take a sheet of paper and write out your wish, then add 'is' or 'are'. For example, 'Beautiful women are ...' or 'A boss of a big company is ...'.

- Say out loud what you have written and finish the sentence with whatever arises in your mind. Write down your answer, even if you think it is completely stupid. Repeat the process several times.

- You will often find that you have one or more negative beliefs about your wish. For example, there will rarely be a woman who doesn't want to be beautiful. However, when you look closely at your deep beliefs about beautiful women you might well find beliefs like 'they are vain' or 'they are arrogant'.

- Sometimes it is enough just to become aware of your half-conscious negative beliefs in order to let them go. For example, it is obvious that not every beautiful

woman is vain or arrogant. Open up to the possibility
that there are some exceptions to your negative beliefs
and that it is those exceptions you are aiming for with
your wish.

- Chuckle at your negative beliefs and make your wish in a
  way that takes care of these doubts. For example, 'I want
  to be beautiful *and* warm-hearted.'

- One of the best ways to align all your subpersonalities
  behind your wish is to focus on how you want to benefit
  others with your wish. If you concentrate on the
  contribution you want to make to the world, surprisingly
  many of your negative voices will quickly give up their
  whingeing.

- Repeat this exercise with another aspect of your wish.
  For example, if you wish for a relationship you can do
  this exercise with 'People in relationships are . . .', 'In a
  relationship I am . . .', 'Women/men are . . .', 'Passionate
  lovers are . . .', 'Married people are . . .'.

- Reformulate your wish until you find an expression that
  you associate effortlessly with very positive views. For
  example, if your desire to look beautiful is hampered by
  some negative associations it might work with something
  like 'I wish to look sexy, attractive and inspiring'.
  Sometimes you have to play around a bit until you have
  your ideal expression.

When my husband and I wanted to move house I did this
exercise for our wish for a great home. To my surprise, I
came up with the idea that 'People who live in a great house
are *enviable*.' Because I really didn't want to be envied I
readjusted my aim and wished for a house that would be
great for my family and myself but didn't necessarily look
like that to others. So the subpersonality in me that is afraid

of envy was appeased and I gained more power to go for my wish even more whole-heartedly. I didn't scold the foolish part in myself who can't deal with envious people. I didn't say to myself, 'Don't be ridiculous, nobody will envy you and if they do you have attracted this envy with your own stupid and negative thoughts.' I didn't even try to fight against this subpersonality in myself because I know that this never works. Instead I accepted myself and tried to find a way to accommodate all my needs. In this way I didn't block my wish from coming true through my half-conscious fears and even felt more positive about my wish.

However, sometimes your inner disagreements cannot be resolved that easily. If you find that you can't readjust your wish in a way that integrates all your subpersonalities you can try the following exercise.

Exercise
Align All Your Subpersonalities to Your Wish

Do this once when you feel strongly torn about your wish

- Arrange two chairs, one for your wish and one for your subpersonality that holds the main negative belief about your wish. For example, you could use one chair for your wish for going out to work as the mother of a baby and one chair for your belief that working mothers are selfish.

- Sit on the first chair and tell your other personality all about your wish and why you want it so badly. For example, tell it about all the advantages of going out to work for yourself and for your baby.

- Swap seats and imagine you are your subpersonality with the negative belief. Tell the other personality why you believe what you believe. For example, tell your other part how selfish it is to want children *and* a career.

- Swap seats again and don't get intimidated. Make your point again and ask the other part what it needs to find a compromise.

- Swap seats another time and start to discuss a compromise. Be honest and only accept what feels like a real compromise.

- Go on swapping seats until you have found a compromise that feels good for both subpersonalities. Remember, such a compromise is always possible. It is in the nature of your inner subpersonalities to be able to find agreements.

- Readjust your wish, so that your whole being with all its subpersonalities can agree on it. You know that this is the case when you feel very good about your wish.

CREATE A FEELING PICTURE IN YOUR MIND

We have already discussed how you can influence the primordial space best through concentration and love. In the next exercise you will learn to use these two faculties of your heart-mind to create a feeling picture in your mind. This feeling picture is the core of the wish-practice method. By creating a feeling picture in your mind you will be working *real* magic because it will enable you to create the miracle of calling things into existence from nowhere.

You have probably heard that it is a good idea to visualise your desired aim. However, 'seeing' things in your mind is not enough – you need to *feel* something as well. Having said that, you don't even need to be able to visualise – it is enough if you *think* about your wish. Creating a feeling picture means holding an image of your wish in your mind (or a thought in case you can't visualise) while *feeling* love, appreciation and all the other wonderful feelings you wish to have once your wish is fulfilled. In this way you are using both love and concentration in the optimal way to influence the primordial ground.

Exercise
Create a Feeling Picture in Your Mind

* Do this for about seven minutes on a daily basis as part of the wish-practice method described at the end of Step 2 (page 107)

- Relax in a way that is convenient for you (perhaps you could use the 'World of happiness' exercise on page 48).

- See in your mind your Higher Consciousness in its most beautiful form and notice how you feel uplifted and loved by its presence. Pray sincerely to your Higher Consciousness, 'Please, show me my heart-wish and guide me to its fulfilment for the best of all beings.'

- Now call to mind your heart-wish and your vision about how you want to contribute to the world through its fulfilment. See everything as clearly as you can in your mind. If you can't imagine everything properly just talk to someone in your mind about how you have achieved your desired aim. Know that your wish has arisen from the primordial ground and feel deep love and appreciation for it. Feel every facet of the wonderful feelings you want to feel once your wish is fulfilled. Be open to discovering new aspects of your heart-wish you haven't thought of before. Stay with your feelings, pictures and thoughts as long as you like, but for a minimum of about seven minutes.

- Say out loud, 'In deepest gratitude – all this or something better now comes easily into existence for the best of all beings.'

Your inner images, feelings and words are the instruments that will lure your desired aim to arise from the primordial ground. If negative pictures and thoughts threaten to over-shadow your experience don't try to fight them. Just don't get hooked on them completely and return over and over again to your positive visualisation, thoughts and feelings. In the next section you will see how to deal with your doubts in a more thorough way.

TRUST THAT YOUR WISH WILL COME TRUE

'Easier said than done,' I hear you grumble.

Let me explain. When we want to influence the primordial ground from which everything arises we need to give it a clear and consistent message. As you probably already know, that is not always easy. What do you think the primordial ground would do with the following message?

> I want to find a soulmate, but I am not sure that this a good idea. I am too old and none of my friends have a great relationship, so it will not be very likely that I will find one. Maybe it would be better to wish to learn to be happy on my own ... but I do need somebody, I really want somebody ... if only the divorce rates were a little bit lower I could believe that even I could succeed. But who would want me? I am not a beauty and have so many idiosyncrasies; I am sure that nobody would put up with them. I want a partner but I just can't believe that anybody could really love me. I have never really been loved before and don't see any reason why that should suddenly change.

Imagine you had a partner who would constantly talk to you like that. Surely you would get fed up with them after some time and question whether you really should continue the relationship.

The primordial ground will not be fed up with anybody when it hears things like this but it will only be able to materialise the strongest message. And the strongest message of the above is 'It is not possible for me to find a partner' and this is what this person will get.

In order to be successful with wish-practice you have to eliminate as many anxieties as possible that your wish might not come true.

'But I can't!' I hear you grumble even louder.

Don't worry, I don't expect you to shed your doubts just like you throw your rubbish in the dustbin. I know that this is not possible. Your doubts are there for a reason, and we have already discussed that fighting against yourself and trying to cut out the pieces you don't like never works. We live with all our subpersonalities (including our doubts) and the only choice we have is whether we live in peace with each other or in war. I suggest that peace is the better option and therefore you need to *convince* your doubts to give up rather than trying to *force* them.

So, at first you need to investigate what your doubts want. What is their purpose? When you look closely you can see that your doubts want to protect you from disappointment. They are not wicked little beings who will laugh nastily if they succeed in making you unhappy. On the contrary, your anxiety and doubts want to help and protect you.

Therefore the first thing you and your doubts need to understand is that there is no real protection from disappointment. You will be disappointed whatever, whether you have not dared to go for your wishes or did go for them but didn't get what you wanted. The disappointment will hurt either way.

If you really understand that you can't protect yourself against hurt and disappointment you might as well take the risk to trust that your highest wish will come true and go for it whole-heartedly. There is always a risk involved if you want to live your dream, in the same way as there is always a risk involved when you start a relationship or when you start your own business. Nothing will give you a guarantee that it will work out. If you want to fulfil your desires you have to be daring, you have to take a risk. Not allowing yourself to trust that your wish will come true is like not allowing yourself to fall in love again. This is not a protection against hurt, but on the contrary, this tactic will bring you much more unhappiness than if you take the risk and go for your dreams.

So, tell your doubts all that and see what they say. If you are lucky, they will already give in a good deal.

The next things you should tell your doubts is that you have a genuine motivation to help others through the fulfilment of your wish. Describe to them your whole vision of how your wish will benefit many, many people and even future generations. You will see that many of your fears will diminish and will be replaced by a deep and genuine feeling that you *do* deserve what you want. This trusting feeling will arise because on a deep level you will sense that there is help for you, that you don't have to make your wishes come true all by yourself.

This help comes from your Higher Consciousness, who can link with you exactly through your altruistic motivation. The more you focus on how you want to benefit others with your wish the more you can expect to be helped by a divine being. I found that to be particularly true in my life. The more I wanted to help others with my own dreams, the more the most unlikely coincidences started to happen, which finally led to the fulfilment of my wish. The discovery of symbol therapy is a good example of that.

Symbol therapy is a form of transpersonal therapy that was given to me in an intuitive way after I had made a wish to find a form of therapy that could cure my clients and myself much more effectively than traditional methods could. I have been trained in several forms of therapy that were the best I knew at the time. But when I was confronted with the horrible problems my clients had to endure I often felt like a Stone Age woman digging in their psyches with blunt tools made of wood and stone. I wasn't totally unsuccessful at it and often my clients were grateful to me. But what I really wanted was a high-tech method that compared to my previous therapeutical methods like a computer compares to Stone Age tools. What's more, I wanted a technique that anybody could quickly learn to use as a self-help method in order not to be dependent on a counsellor or therapist any more.

With 'discovering' symbol therapy my wish came true in every detail. I rarely use any of my previous methods any more because symbol therapy does the job so beautifully in a fraction of the time. Many times I have had clients with severe and chronic disorders that they had tried to treat in years of therapy. With symbol therapy they cured *themselves* within weeks.

So, back to your fears and doubts. If you find that they don't want to give up, no matter how hard you try to convince them, you can work with symbol therapy in order to overcome them. You do that by visualising or sensing a healing symbol in your heart that was given to you by your own Higher Consciousness. When your inner obstacles are confronted with the wonderful love and wisdom radiating from your healing symbol they will melt away willingly and your wish-fulfilling gem will sparkle with more radiance than ever, ready to bring anything into existence that you want.

Exercise
Symbol Therapy for Overcoming Your Doubts

Do Part 1 once
*Do Part 2 for two minutes on a daily basis as part of the
wish-practice method and every time you start to worry that
your wish might not come true*

Part 1

Do once:

- Summarise your wish into one or two sentences and
  don't forget the part about how you want to contribute
  to the world with your wish. Then picture your wish as
  vividly as you can.

- Measure on a scale how much you believe that your wish
  will come true. A zero is not believing at all and a ten is
  fully believing.

- Relax in the way that is convenient to you. (You can use
  the relaxation at the beginning of the 'World of happiness' exercise on page 48.)

- When you are in deep relaxation, you are ready to come
  into contact with your Higher Consciousness, who will
  help you to overcome all your fears and doubts. See your
  Higher Consciousness as an angelic being surrounded by
  light, or as a beautiful shimmering light that has a living
  and loving quality. Feel how you are embraced by the
  love and support of your Higher Consciousness.

- Ask your Higher Consciousness, 'Can you please give me
  a healing-symbol to overcome my suffering that comes
  from not trusting that my wish will come true, for the
  best of all beings.'

- You might be shown one or several symbols (for

example, flowers, gems or geometrical forms) and you should pick one that you find attractive and has a beautiful and bright colour. Acknowledge the very first thought or idea of a symbol that comes into your mind. If you are not sure whether you have received the right symbol you can check with your Higher Consciousness. Watch for an inner feeling of 'yes' or 'no'.

- When you have received a healing-symbol you feel good about thanking your Higher Consciousness for its help.

- Say to yourself, 'I always love myself deeply with all my weaknesses and even if I can't trust that my wish will come true.'

- Visualise your healing-symbol in the middle of your chest in your heart, and when you breathe out exhale the colour of your symbol throughout your body, into the surrounding of your body and into your world. When you breathe in just enjoy the presence of your symbol in your heart. Then exhale the colour and the positive qualities of your symbol again. Do this *in a loving way* for two minutes. Then open your eyes again.

Part 2

Daily practice:

- Visualise or feel your healing-symbol in your heart and breathe out its colour and good qualities in a loving way for two minutes a day as part of your daily wish-practice method and whenever you start to worry that your wish will not come true. Always start by saying, 'I always love myself deeply with all my weaknesses and even if I can't trust that my wish will come true.' Visualise your symbol in *exactly* the form it was given to you by your Higher Consciousness and never change it yourself. If it seems to change on its own accord don't allow this to happen but always go back to its original form.

- Measure how much you believe that your wish will come true on the scale of belief once every fortnight. Over time the number on the scale will slowly creep up.

By practising your healing symbol regularly you will be able to remove the biggest obstacle that is in the way of making your wish come true, which is lack of faith. It might take a few days or even a few weeks until you can fully feel the effects of working with your healing symbol but the effort will be worth it.

When you measure seven or eight on the scale of belief it will be enough if you use your healing symbol only if you start worrying again. Symbol therapy is completely safe and has been proven in many hundreds of cases.

A close friend of mine started to work for herself six years ago and the first two years went very well. Then, suddenly and completely out of the blue, all requests from her clients stopped and no matter how hard she tried she just couldn't generate new business. My friend was a single mother with two girls to support and you can imagine how worried and bad she felt. When her bad stretch had lasted several months she thought seriously about returning to an employed job, a prospect she disliked thoroughly. At that point I told her how she could use symbol therapy in order to overcome her anxieties and strengthen her belief that her business would pick up again.

My friend willingly gave symbol therapy a try. As soon as she started to practise with her healing symbol her fears lessened drastically and she was able to wait patiently for better times while living off her savings. She met two colleagues who had given up in a similar situation and had returned to the security (and drudgery) of an employed job. But my friend became more and more convinced that everything would work out fine for her. And so it was. After a very bad stretch of six months and a moderately bad stretch for another nine months her business did pick up; for over two years now she has been making much more money than she needs to maintain her family. She told me that without the help of her symbols she would never have had the stamina to go through this bad time and would have lost the business that she loved so much.

Faith is a wonderful power that will carry you far, and with symbol therapy you know how you can maintain it. Whenever your doubts and anxieties creep up, don't dwell on them but breathe the colour of your symbol *in a loving way* into your body and its surrounding. Nothing changes and transforms obstacles like love (and nothing is more futile than trying to fight them).

Before I finish this section let me give you some more advice on how to strengthen your belief that your wish will come true: the most important is to practise selective attention! Instead of focusing on all the people who *don't* have what you want, watch out for those who *do* have what you want. And then watch out for those who have had similar terrible childhoods and disadvantaged backgrounds as you and succeeded nevertheless, and for those who are even less intelligent, beautiful, strong (or whatever else) than you. If they are all successful you can be as well. Think also about all the wishes in your own life that have already come true instead of constantly thinking about the ones that haven't come true (yet!).

If you want to have a miracle in your life, read books about miracles, talk to people who have experienced miracles and go to workshops that promise miracles. Even if these workshops can't deliver these miracles straight away you will probably learn a lot and meet like-minded, inspiring and supportive people. The more you fill your awareness with proof that it is possible to get what you want (even for someone as disadvantaged as you!) the stronger your faith in yourself and into the fulfilment of your wish will grow.

One last word: if you have successfully built up your faith into the fulfilment of your wish you need to take good care that your newly found trust will not be damaged or even completely destroyed.

Don't talk to anybody about your wish who doesn't believe that it will come true! Don't look for support for your wishes from people who don't believe that you fully deserve your wish.

Nothing will destroy your faith quicker than people who think that you are unrealistic, selfish, crazy or downright stupid. Don't let this happen. Don't talk to anybody about any of your wishes unless you are very sure that they will be fully supportive. In an extreme case this means that you have to pursue your wishes totally unsupported by the people around you. Don't let this discourage you. As time goes by you will find more like-minded people who want the same things in life as you and who will give you the support and inspiration you need.

CREATE SYMBOLS OF YOUR WISH

Step 2 seems like a lot of doing and some people might groan about all the exercises. But believe me, when you come to letting go of your craving and are confronted with the task of non-doing, you would be glad if you could still do some more little exercises instead of simply trying to be serene and patient.

On a deeper level the mind is much more impressed by symbols than by words. This is why religions give us their symbols and why big brands give us their logos. Once our minds have latched on to these symbols a strong dynamic is set in motion; this deepens our religious bonds on the one hand and makes us buy only certain brands on the other. In wish-practice we can use the same mechanism and pull our deep subconscious mind towards our desired aim by creating our own symbols.

Exercise
Create a Collage About Your Wish

*Do this once

- Take a pile of glossy magazines, cut out any pictures that depict your wish and create a beautiful collage with them. You can also add the occasional word if you don't find an appropriate image. As always, don't forget the part about how you want to contribute to the world with your wish.

- Find a picture that shows and symbolises your Higher Consciousness and paste it in the middle of your collage.

- Write underneath your collage 'For the best of all beings'.

- Hang the collage in a place where you can see it frequently and look at it for as long and as often as you like. Enjoy the prospect that everything you see on it will come true one day.

- Alternatively you can buy or create symbols of your wish. For example, buy a house made of china that looks exactly like the house you would like to live in. Put these symbols in a special place in your home.

Since I have started to make collages my wish-practice has become much more effective. I can say that for sure because my collages have provided me with valuable feedback about how much my life has changed. When I look at them now I find it unbelievable how much my life has improved. The collages were full of pictures of aims that were completely out of reach for me at the time. I hadn't just used images of myself a little bit happier but I had asked for drastic changes for my body, my emotions, finances, relationships, career and spiritual development.

In the last ten years I have worked through four different collages, making each one more bold and outrageous than the one before. It is one of my favourite leisure pursuits to gaze at my newest collage and look forward to its fulfilment. Remember, I am no more talented at making my wishes come true than anybody else. If I can do it, you can do it as well.

MAKE A DECLARATION TO THE UNIVERSE

What symbols do for our deep subconscious mind, words do for our conscious mind. On a conscious level we are more impressed by words than by symbols. For example, if your daughter has been naughty you don't show her quietly some highly meaningful symbols – no, you *tell* her off.

Words are the missing link between the images that have arisen from the primordial ground and the material plane. This is literally true: physicists have measured the frequency of vibration in the sounds of words and found that it is just between the frequency of vibration of material things and the vibration of colours and images. This means that once you have formed strong ideas and images the spoken word will give your wishes the final push into the material world.

However, it isn't as easy as it sounds. In order to use the power of your words successfully they need to have a certain strength. If you speak with a feeble and quivering voice like a little mouse your words can hardly call things into existence, nor can words spoken by somebody who frequently tells lies.

If you want to use words to make your wishes come true,

first of all you need integrity. That means that whatever you say can be 100 per cent relied on. If you tell lies your word will be literally broken and not very useful for wish-practice. In order to make your wishes come true you need to create a habit in which everything you say will come true. I mean *everything*! If you say you will phone her, do it! If you say you will be there to help him, be there! And if you say you will deliver the work by next week, stick to it! Don't say things to please people and than conveniently forget them afterwards. If you really can't stick to what you have agreed on let the other person know and apologise. With every promise you keep and with every situation in which you can be relied on, your words will gain in power and so will your wish-practice.

Swearing, calling people names and saying vicious things is not a good idea either (as tempting as it sometimes is). If you want to use your words for wish-practice, keeping to a certain hygiene of speech will be as helpful as keeping to your dental hygiene in order to avoid the dentist.

And watch out about the way you complain to other people about your unfair destiny, the appalling lack of love in other people and the general misery of the world. I like a good moan when things don't go the way I want them to because it feels so good to let off some steam. But be aware that you can easily go too far in this direction. Do you remember how I always told everybody that 'I would never get what I needed'? This is a typical example of negative wish-practice. I only started to get what I needed once I had completely given up saying things like that. And I only found a real soulmate after I had stopped bitching about men.

Words are powerful – they can hurt you more than phys-ical pain and equally they can make you happier than the most beautiful material things. And words can manifest with astounding speed. If you tell a small child whose mind is still open and unprotected what amazing talents he has, the chances are that the child will quickly manifest the first signs of just those talents. Sadly, this dynamic works exactly in the same way the other way around. A child who is called 'naughty' and 'bad' often enough will quickly become like that and stay like that.

However, as adults we can't use the same technique to call forward the most amazing qualities in ourselves as long as we haven't worked on a deeper level to remove our faulty beliefs. This is the reason why affirmations usually don't work. If you don't believe them deep down you just create an inner war by trying to hammer them into your head. And if you *do* believe them you don't need to repeat them over and over again in order to convince your subconscious mind. You only need to say them once and with conviction and soon they will manifest.

The most famous example of the power of the word was nobody less than Jesus Christ. 'Get up and walk,' he said to Lazarus, and so he did. Jesus spoke these words of magic with authority and conviction and this is why they worked.

If you want to use the power of your word to make your wishes come true you first need to work on the level of your ideas and beliefs, and make sure that your whole being is whole-heartedly behind your wish as explained earlier. Then you can move on to make a declaration to the universe.

Exercise
Make a Declaration to the Universe

*Do this once or as often as you like

- Plan for this declaration to be a special moment. You can create a little ceremony with candles, incense and prayer, or you can go to a special place like the top of hill where you have a wonderful view. Be imaginative and find a place and a time that suits your needs, and will give your declaration the solemnity that you find appropriate.

- When you have arrived at your special place or in the middle of your ceremony imagine all the divine beings in front of you. They smile at you with love and they express their wish to help you.

- Read out your wish-list, including how you want to feel on all levels once your wish is fulfilled, what you want to stop and how you want to benefit others with your wish.

- Then say to your Higher Consciousness and to the whole universe with conviction and authority:

  Higher Consciousness, I align myself with you as the most powerful positive force in the universe and I ask you for your help. I declare that all this or something better comes now easily into existence for the highest unfolding of myself and all beings. I am effortlessly making every change in myself and in my environment that is necessary to reach my aim. I am open and I look forward to receiving and enjoying all these wonderful gifts.

- Think and feel that your declaration reaches every corner of the whole universe and reverberates through its entire vastness. Know that it will connect with everybody who can help you with your wish and who will benefit from it, and that it will draw them effortlessly towards you.

- Finish your little ceremony in a way that feels good and appropriate to you.

Let me explain in more detail what each part of this declaration means:

- *'Create a little ceremony ...'* This will give your unconscious mind and the universe a message that you are serious.

You are not making your declaration in a flippant way –
no, you really mean what you have to say.

- *'Say with conviction and authority ...'* You have power and it
is transmitted through your word. Don't mutter and
murmur or speak anxiously with a quivering voice. You
are in charge now, speak up!

- *'Higher Consciousness, I align myself with you ...'* You try to
become one with the most positive force in the universe in
order to make your wishes as wise and as powerful as
possible.

- *'and I ask you for your help ...'* Although you are powerful
you acknowledge that you could do with some help and
you ask it from the most loving and intelligent source that
is available to you.

- *'I declare ...'* You *are* powerful, so make your wish wisely.

- *'all this or something better...'* This is a security clause in case
you haven't made your wish in a completely wise way. It
gives the primordial space and the divine beings the possibility to provide you with something better.

- *'comes now easily into existence ...'* You don't want a lot of
trouble trying to achieve your aim and you don't want to
have any time delay, do you? So you had better make that
clear right from the start.

- *'for the highest unfolding of myself and all beings ...'* This is
your altruistic motivation that is so essential in wish-
practice because it is the only way to achieve the happiness
that you desire.

- *'I am effortlessly making every change in myself and in my environment ...'* You and your life have to change in order to
accomplish your dreams. However, you don't want these
changes to be strenuous or painful.

- '*And I am open ...*' You are ready to receive your wish and you are open to it coming to you in surprising and unexpected ways.

- '*and I look forward to receiving and enjoying ...*' You are even allowed to enjoy it!

- '*all these wonderful gifts.*' No matter how powerful your declaration, ultimately your wish can only come to you like a gift and you need a humble and grateful attitude to receive it.

Let me tell you the story of how Roger used a declaration to the universe to find his soulmate.

Roger had been single for many years and slowly, slowly he had started to give up hope. He had had girlfriends, but nobody he wanted to marry. However, marriage was what he wanted with all his heart. One day he talked to a friend about his dilemma and she asked him whether he had already made his declaration to the universe. When Roger said 'No', she started to tell him off a bit and asked him strictly how he thought he could ever expect to find his partner if he hadn't even made his declaration.

Roger took her advice to heart and a few days later he made a sincere declaration while he went on a walk. Three weeks (!) later he met a woman and after only a very short time he knew for sure that he had found the woman he wanted to marry.

PRACTISE THE WISH-PRACTICE METHOD

If you have followed everything so far, you know what you want, you feel very positive about it and you have an altruistic vision of how you want to contribute to the world with your wish. You have also done a bit of soul-searching and you have successfully removed negative views about your wish. Then you have learnt to decrease doubts about the fulfilment of your wish through symbol therapy and how to create a feeling picture in your mind. To support the process you have created symbols of your wish and you have made a declaration to the universe. Well done!

Now we will put all this together in order to practise the wish-practice method. In only fifteen minutes a day you will be practising the essentials that are necessary to lure your desired aim from the primordial ground into existence. You can even do this practice while lying in bed, so you cannot complain it is too much work. First I will give you a summary, then I will describe the wish-practice method in detail.

Summary of the Wish-practice Method

Stage 1
Relax (about three minutes).
Stage 2
Feel the love and the appreciation of your Higher Consciousness (about three minutes).
Stage 3
Create a feeling picture in your mind (about seven minutes).
Stage 4
Work with your healing symbol (about two minutes).

Exercise
The Wish-practice Method

*Do this daily for fifteen minutes

Stage 1: Relaxation

- Put on a piece of soft and romantic music. As you enjoy the beautiful music relax more and more. Let yourself go with every out-breath and relax your whole being. Do this for about three minutes.

Stage 2: Feel the Love and Appreciation of Your Higher Consciousness

- See in your mind your Higher Consciousness in its most beautiful form and feel that it is sending you love and appreciation. Deeply enjoy these positive feelings and give them back to your Higher Consciousness so that you become a union of love and happiness. Do this for about three minutes. Then pray sincerely to your Higher Consciousness, 'Please show me my heart-wish and guide me to its fulfilment for the best of all beings.'

Stage 3: Create a Feeling Picture in Your Mind

- See in your mind a beautiful gate with the inscription 'The fulfilment of my heart's desire'. As you step through this gate see and feel that all your deep wishes are fulfilled. Include in your inner vision how you want to contribute to the world through the fulfilment of your desires. See everything as clearly as you can in your mind. If you can't visualise, just hear yourself talking to someone about how you have achieved your desired aim. Feel every facet of the wonderful feelings you want to feel once your wish is fulfilled. Be open to discovering new aspects of your heart-wish you haven't thought of before. Stay with your feelings, pictures and thoughts as long as you like, but for a minimum of seven minutes. Say out loud, 'In deepest gratitude – all this or something better now comes easily into existence for the best of all beings.'

Stage 4: Practise Your Healing Symbol

- Start by telling yourself, 'I always love myself deeply with all my weaknesses and even if I can't trust that my wish will come true.' Visualise your healing symbol in the middle of your chest in your heart and when you breathe out exhale the colour of your symbol throughout your body, into the surroundings of your body and into your world. Do this *in a loving way* for two minutes. (Always visualise your symbol in exactly the form and colour it was given to you by your Higher Consciousness. Never allow it to change of its own accord and never change it yourself.)

- Finish the wish-practice method by saying, 'May all the good from my practice go to all beings and bring them ultimate happiness.'

Explanation of the Wish-practice Method

In the wish-practice method there is one prayer and two declarations. They are all extremely important because they are like a security fence around your wish-practice. They will help you to stay connected to the source of deepest wisdom and happiness that is available to you, and they will affirm your altruistic motivation in order to avoid wasting time and energy on wishes that will not bring you the satisfaction you desire.

In **Stage 1** you will relax deeply in order to open up to your inner being and to your Higher Consciousness.

In **Stage 2** you will come into contact with your Higher Consciousness. Remember that you can imagine it in whatever form suits you. It is fine just to think of a beautiful light that has an intelligent and loving quality. In its essence the Higher Consciousness is the same for all of us – it is the source of all the highest love and the highest wisdom of the whole universe.

It is essential to let the love of your Higher Consciousness into your heart even if you sometimes feel unworthy. Only if you allow yourself to be loved will you allow yourself to receive the fulfilment of your wishes. You will also send love back to your Higher Consciousness until you feel like one union of happiness and bliss. This union of yourself and your Higher Consciousness is the highest development of human existence, and the more you can progress on this path the happier you will be and the easier it will be for you to make your wishes come true.

Then you will go on to make a prayer to your Higher Consciousness and ask it to show you your heart-wish and to guide you to its fulfilment for the best of all beings. This prayer is important. If you are like most people you will discover that your wishes will evolve as you develop yourself. And the higher your wishes are the more happiness and fulfilment they can bring to you and others.

Be open to discovering new aspects of your wish you have never thought of before. Maybe your wish will change altogether. You can let this happen; you don't need to visualise exactly the same images every day. What counts is that you feel positive and deeply inspired by your practice.

In **Stage 3** you will walk through a magic gate into the area of 'the fulfilment of your heart's desire', and there you will find that your deepest wishes have come true. Stepping through this imaginary gate will help you to open up to even more wonderful possibilities. Let all this happen in the knowledge that you can *create* reality. You can even see yourself flying, if you want, without having to worry that this isn't 'realistic' enough.

You can just leave all the practicalities to the primordial ground and to your Higher Consciousness to sort out. See everything in your mind that you wish for and feel all the feelings that you want to feel once your wish is fulfilled. If you want a loving relationship *feel* loved right now. If you want to be healed *feel* your radiantly healthy body right now. You can evoke any feelings in your heart-mind by pretending and imagining them. The more you can feel these feelings and see these images, and the longer you can rest in them, the better. Finish the third stage by making your first declaration, 'In deepest gratitude – all this or something better now comes easily into existence for the best of all beings.'

Wish-practice is a mixture of the exertion of your own personal power on the one hand and of the grace of your Higher Consciousness on the other. Your declaration mirrors this mixture. You say 'in deepest gratitude' to honour your Higher Consciousness and to thank it for its help, and you say the rest of your declaration as an expression of your personal power. However, please don't forget that our Higher Consciousness and we ourselves are essentially one and the same. The more we can realise this and the more we understand that the essence of our being is the primordial ground itself, the more powerful our wish-practice will become. Until then we can rely more on the help and the grace of our Higher Consciousness.

In **Stage 4** you can visualise your healing-symbol if you experience a feeling of worry that your wish might not come true. Symbol therapy will help you reliably to overcome this major obstacle in wish-practice.

Before you visualise your healing-symbol always say to yourself, 'I always love myself deeply with all my weaknesses and even if I can't trust that my wish will come true.' This statement will help you to overcome the block of wanting to change yourself too fast and too violently. I can't repeat often enough: you can't change yourself like you can screw up a part of a badly written essay in order to start a new one. You can't change yourself like you can cut out the rotten bits of an apple or paint over a half-finished painting. Human beings can't be improved through aggression and not even through good resolutions.

Change will only occur through genuine insight and through a feeling of being deeply accepted and loved just as you are. When you can give this love to yourself you will be connected with your heart and its genuine wisdom. This – and only this – will bring about lasting change and improvements to all your problems, weaknesses and failures.

Visualise and breathe the colour and good qualities of your healing-symbols and don't forget to breathe in a loving way. Again, it is the love that will help to unlock the blocks in your subconscious mind.

After breathing the colour of your symbol you can move on to your final declaration and dedicate all the good of your practice to the benefit of all beings.

If you find that all these prayers and dedications are getting a bit much now, remember one more time the dreadful destiny of the White family. Think of everything that is or was horrible in your own life or in the life of anybody else. In Buddhism we are taught that all this suffering has developed at its deepest root through one single cause, and that is selfishness and absence of an altruistic motivation. And Buddhist teachers go on to say that the most important thing to improve our life is wishing and working for the benefit of *all* beings and not only for ourselves.

It is best to do these fifteen minutes of wish-practice in an undisturbed place. You can even do this while lying in bed. Just make sure that you don't fall asleep after the first thirty seconds and really try to enjoy the practice. Don't become so bitterly sincere about the whole process that you get wrinkles on your forehead from concentrating too strongly. It will not make your wishes come true faster and it doesn't look good either. Instead, practise with a smile of genuine enjoyment on your face, which will be beneficial for your wish-practice as well as for your beautiful youthful looks.

One last word: don't carry out the wish-practice method more often than twice a day because otherwise you can easily fall into the trap of thinking that it is only you who is making everything happen. But wish-practice is more like sowing seeds that must be left in peace a lot of the time to sprout and to develop into beautiful plants. In the same way your wishes will grow and unfold, and if you try to force them into existence you will harvest nothing but disappointment.

STEP 2, STRENGTHENING YOUR WISH-POWER: THE ESSENTIALS

In Step 2 you learned how to use and to strengthen the tools of your heart-mind in order to attract what you want. These tools are clear ideas, concentrated thoughts, love, prayer, faith, humour, inner images, symbols and the power of your words.

- Write a precise wish-list, including:

  1. Every detail of your wish.
  2. How you want to contribute to the world with your wish in every possible detail.
  3. How you want to feel on all levels when your wish is fulfilled.
  4. What you want to avoid in the area of your wish.
  5. A short summary of the two or three most important and unnegotiable aspects of your wish.

- Find out about your subconscious negative beliefs and let them go through humour or reasoning, or through a dialogue with the subpersonality that holds a negative belief about your wish.

- Learn how to create a feeling picture in your mind.

- Strengthen your trust that your wish will come true:

  1. Through focusing on how you want to contribute to the world with your wish.
  2. Through practising selective attention and wise communication.
  3. Through using symbol therapy for wish-practice.

- Create symbols of your wish by making a collage.

- Strengthen the power of your word and make a declaration to the universe.

- Practise the wish-practice method for fifteen minutes on a daily basis.

Step 3

Taking Action

Imagine if it were true that the universe owed us a nice life. Wouldn't that be a horrible thought? It would be absolutely maddening to think that all that went wrong in our lives, every circumstance where we have been disadvantaged, had happened *despite* the fact that the universe owed us a nice life. 'Why can it be,' we would rant and rage, 'that everybody, yes everybody, has what I ought to have, too? Why have I been left out from my fair share of the gorgeous cream cake that everybody is munching with such a smug pleasure?'

Thank goodness it isn't true that the universe owes us a nice life. How liberating to know that it doesn't owe us anything at all. We are not helpless victims at the mercy of a random and unfair God who gives to some of His children while viciously neglecting the others.

The truth is that we are in charge of our destiny ourselves, that it was we who created all the bad and good things in our lives ourselves. This thought is not really flattering when we look at the unfortunate things in our lives. But it can make us deservedly proud of ourselves when we think of what is working and good.

The universe owes us nothing and therefore *we* can create a wonderful life for ourselves and for everybody who wants to come along with us. We can create whatever we want from the primordial ground. However, on a relative level, we live in a world that already exists and we have to obey its law, which is primarily the law of karma. This says that we get back whatever we give out.

Many people agree on the idea of karma but they don't necessarily act on it. They are passive and they are waiting for problems to be solved all by themselves of their own accord. If things don't go the way they wish they are depressed or angry and demand to be treated in a better way, conveniently forgetting that it was they themselves who set up the conditions for everything in their lives.

I don't want to blame them, as I myself am often like that. I guess everybody is – it is another trait of being human that we like to blame others for our own misery.

However, if we want to make our big wishes come true we need to learn to act radically on the idea of karma and put it into practice as well as we can. Most importantly, we need to understand that we have to give out what we want to get and that we need to create the conditions ourselves that will lead to the fulfilment of our wish. In other words – we need to get up from our comfortable sofa and do something.

When you work to make your wishes come true you need to be completely committed to them and to do everything that common sense dictates to you. You need to study, to work, to find help and to search in every possible way, just as you would do if you had never heard anything about wish-practice. Working with the wish-practice method, sadly, is *not* a substitute for doing all these things. However, the practice will make sure that all your working will be crowned with success.

But before you now either throw this book away because it sounds like too much effort, or plunge into a frenzy of benevolent doing that leaves you totally exhausted, read the next section.

ENJOY THE PROCESS

With regard to work attitudes, there are two categories of people and you need to decide for yourself which category you tend to belong to. These are: lazybones and workaholics.

Lazybones spend too much time in front of the television, procrastinate and basically never get anything done. Workaholics, on the other hand, burn themselves out, get on the nerves of other people with their constant activity, and think everyone and everything depends only on them. Both sorts of people have to learn how to *enjoy* working for their wish in a consistent and organised way.

Lazybones need to have the experience that they are actually able to achieve something and that it is highly satisfying to set themselves tasks and to work in an organised way. Workaholics need to learn to relax and enjoy while they are working, and not to regard themselves as so important and to think that everything depends on them. They need to understand that wish-practice is only partly their own doing and that the rest is magic and grace.

It is easy to work enthusiastically for your wish when it is new and you haven't experienced any major obstacles yet. But making wishes come true can sometimes take a long time and if you have tired yourself out too quickly you will soon become exhausted and frustrated. And the more frustrated you are the more difficult it will be to be successful with wish-practice. When you are in a bad mood you can't give the primordial ground those consistently positive messages that are so important; this will make you (sorry to say) less attractive. So, staying in a good mood is crucial while you are working for your wish.

The process of losing weight is a perfect example to illustrate this point. If you try a crash diet you will quickly come to the point where you bitterly resent having had to starve yourself while everybody else seems to be tucking in with gusto without ever putting on a gram. Then you start bingeing with a terribly bad conscience and soon your weight will be higher than before and your mood will hit rock bottom. This is *not* how you should approach making your wishes come true and neither is it the way to lose weight.

When I was a counsellor for addictions I specialised in eating disorders and I ran many courses for people who wanted to lose weight. The way I taught them to lose weight mirrors exactly the way I will show you how to make any wish come true. My method worked: everybody lost weight, could hold their lower weight effortlessly and most of all *enjoyed* the process.

I taught my clients only a few simple things. At first I told them that they could trust their body and that it would tell them exactly what and how much to eat in order to become and stay slim. The most important slimming guidelines were to eat only when they were *genuinely* hungry, which meant they had to learn to recognise the hunger feeling that came from their stomach rather than from their mouth.

Then I told them to forget anything they had ever heard about slimming food and to eat *exactly* what they felt like eating, to recognise when they were full and to stop eating at that point. The next meal would be no sooner or later than the next signs of genuine hunger. No exercise required and no cutting out of sweets or fat!

This approach is so startlingly simple that at first I was regularly met with disbelief. But it works! People who successfully lost weight and stayed slim *without any effort* eat exactly in this way and so do people who have never had any weight problems. If you don't believe me ask all your slim friends. Our body has an interest in staying slim and when we follow its impulses we can achieve our ideal weight in the easiest and most enjoyable way possible.

The same is true for wish-practice. In the same way as you can trust your body to guide you to your perfect weight, so you can trust your heart-mind to show you the wishes that will lead to happiness. If you then work for your wishes with some basic but enjoyable discipline you are bound to have success because you can maintain this discipline for a long time if necessary. This is not to say that every wish takes years to come true, but if it does you need to be able to take on the challenge. This will only be possible if you can stay in a good mood throughout the process and never work so hard that you exhaust yourself completely and never be so lazy that you don't do what is required.

But one little word of warning: working for your wish in an enjoyable way doesn't mean that you will never encounter any fear. On the contrary, stepping beyond your usual limitations will almost always bring up some anxiety. But, so what?! If you know that fears are a sign that you are really moving on you can even enjoy them! The best way to gain confidence and to overcome your anxiety is to think of all the people you want to benefit with your wish. It is so much easier to be brave for others than merely for yourself.

When I was about to give my first public talk I was nearly sick because I felt anxious. I even yelled at my husband, which has never happened before or since. But should I have let this fear stop me? Certainly not! There were all these people waiting who had come to listen to my talk and thinking about them helped me to give my talk *despite* my own nervousness. The next talks I gave were already much easier and these days I really enjoy them.

'How do I know if I work in the right way for my wish?' somebody might ask.

If you like exercise think of the way you would climb a mountain as a leisure activity. It is an effort but a really enjoyable one. It can be scary but that is part of the fun. If you hate sport think of a creative hobby – you have to concentrate but it is so much pleasure as well. You might be worried that you are not able to make what you want but this fear doesn't stop you. This is the way to work for your wishes – with enjoyable effort and a brave mind that doesn't shy away from taking some risks. With this guideline in mind you can move on to Step 3.

GIVE OUT WHAT YOU WANT TO GET

Give out what you want to get sounds like the advice of your pious auntie Mary and some people might argue that they have done that for years and never had *anything* back. I agree that sometimes it can feel as if you are the *only* loving person in the whole world, surrounded by no one but ungrateful, mean and egotistical monsters. Your pious auntie Mary would probably say that this is all your fault because your giving was still not selfless enough and that it is wrong to expect anything back. I disagree with your auntie.

If you want to make your wishes come true you need to make your own well-being *as* important as that of other people (not *more* important, just *as* important). With that thought in mind you might want to stop giving to the egotistical monsters and start to give to people where you have a chance that something will come back to you. Giving what you want to get does *not* mean throwing your pearls before swine. Auntie Mary would probably be shocked about so much selfishness but has she ever achieved her dreams? Is she the kind of person who makes other people feel good about themselves and supports them to achieve their full potential? I don't think so. Auntie Mary is probably exactly the kind of person who has suppressed her own wishes all her life and has become pretty bitter over it.

The law of karma says that we have to give what we want to receive, but we really don't have to beat ourselves up to follow that rule. That way our giving will become more enjoyable, and as always it is our genuine feeling that counts. If you start to work for a charity in order to obey this law, but you do it with clenched teeth and while continuously pitying yourself because none of your efforts will ever be recognised, then not much will come back to you. But if you can greet your neighbour with a friendly smile, and because you are in a good mood offer to water his plants while he is on holiday, he might well help you some other time in an important way. It is not so much the watering of the plants that counts but your genuine friendliness.

Being altruistic doesn't mean that you have to go against your natural inclination. On the contrary, to be loving and giving is the essence of our being and the more we can come into alignment with these natural positive impulses the easier our wish-practice will be and the happier we will feel.

Generally speaking we have to put *something* out there to get something back. And the more you do that with a positive state of mind the better. What about telling your wife how beautiful she is and what about telling your husband how much you admire his work? That would be a good start. In our culture most people don't lack material resources as much as they lack self-confidence. Almost everybody craves to hear that they are doing well and that they are looking good. Be generous – tell them!

You can't always expect that you will get things back from the same person you gave to – on the contrary this tactic can actually lead to the opposite of what you want. If a wife, for example, gives more and more to her husband in the silent hope that at some point he might notice and start giving something back she will often be bitterly disappointed. If the dear husband is not willing or able to give anything back all this receiving will actually work like a mounting debt for him, which will make him more resentful rather than grateful. It would be wiser for the wife to ask him directly to do something for her and to deal with whatever he replies.

Giving out what you want to get means giving in a skilful way to people who appreciate your giving so that a positive circle is set into motion.

It is also a good idea to give in the field in which you want to receive. If you want to have more love in your life be more loving generally. If you want a promotion be more appreciative about your colleagues. If you want to have more money, give more money to charity. But if you now complain that you would have even less money if you did then you still haven't understood the law of karma. You *will* get back what you give and often much more than that. It's the law and you can rely on it! The only trouble with this rule is that you never know *when and how* you will get something back. The ways of karma are so intricate and so mysterious that they can seem completely random. But they are not. The good things in your life happen for no other reason than your own beneficial doing in the nearer or further past.

Remember for a moment how you want to contribute to the world with your wish. It is wonderful if you can put your altruistic motivation into practice now. If you want to benefit a lot of people with your products and service, start now by supplying your friends and family with what you have to offer. If you want to be a great musician, start to make a few people happy with your music. But please make sure that you only give to those people who appreciate you and who support your wish because otherwise you will just undermine yourself.

This is the way many high achievers started to work in their field. They focused on what they loved to do and on how to benefit others, and the appreciation, the money and the fame they finally gained grew from there as a by-product, so to speak. Of course there have also been plenty of rich and famous people who were less altruistic. However, one thing is sure – they certainly were much less happy and fulfilled than more altruistic people.

Whatever you want, always act and speak accordingly and never do anything that could sabotage your wish. If you want to have better relationships, don't speak badly about your friends behind their backs. Even if they can't hear you right now, the law of karma will make sure that they will turn against you some day for seemingly no apparent reason.

So, always keep in mind giving out what you want to get, even if the people and circumstances seem completely disconnected. Your friendly but relentless karma accountant will book everything you did into your accounts and you can be sure that you will get your fair share, be it positive or negative. Karma is neither punishment nor reward – it's simply the way the universe works.

DON'T DO IT ALONE

Many people are fond of the idea of a self-made millionaire – more likely a billionaire these days. We like the thought that we could rise from being a dish-washer to a billionaire just through our own effort and without any outside help.

However, there is no such thing as a self-made billionaire. This idea is just a myth. There is no self-made spiritual enlightenment; there is no self-made successful business and no self-made successful anybody. Everybody who is achieving in their field has had help in a multitude of forms. The average billionaire, for example, usually has a partner for emotional support and to take care of the domestic arrangements. Almost certainly there would be supportive and intelligent business-partners, background funding and many more things that helped pave the way to success.

It is similar if your aim is spiritual development. I am always astonished at how many people think they can progress on the spiritual path without the guidance of an experienced and qualified teacher. These same people would never attempt to learn to play the piano or to speak a foreign language without a teacher of some kind. But in the most difficult field of human development they are confident that they can find out everything by themselves through the method of trial and error. Unfortunately, in this

way they will never become any more successful than the
musician who never had a lesson and the lawyer who never
went to law school.

**If you want to make your dream come true seek out the
help of people who are more experienced than you.**

Some people think it is a positive sign if they are able to do
more and more things without any outside help, but I don't
completely agree. People who are trying to become more
and more autonomous are often going down a dead-end
street because they are cutting themselves off from all their
nourishing sources. On the other side, everybody will
progress in their field of choice many times faster if they are
able to recruit the help of more experienced people. It is
much more effective to learn from mentors, models and
teachers than through your own failures. And it hurts much
less then going down the painful route of learning through
emotional crisis, business bankruptcy and divorce.

Most people are happy to pass on some helpful tips when
they are approached in a respectful and appreciative way.
This is something I learnt from my husband Nigel. When he
was doing some post-graduate research he wrote a draft
paper of about thirty pages. Then he did something that I
found quite bold. He tracked down the e-mail addresses of
all the leading international experts in his field, sent them
his paper and asked for feedback.

I really thought these people would consider themselves
too important to take the time and effort to read through
thirty pages written by an unknown post-graduate student,
let alone giving him detailed feedback about it. How wrong
I was! Nigel got several very friendly letters back, including
detailed and constructive feedback on his work.

My own success is due to the help of my Buddhist and
psychotherapeutic teachers and of my friends, from whom I
learnt everything that was important on my way. And this
journey is by no means finished yet. It is one of my greatest

joys to encounter people from whom I can learn something that helps me further.

When you look for people who might be able to help you to make your wish come true it is important to communicate in a way that inspires them to work with you. How motivated would you feel to help somebody who says, '*I* want to be rich, *I* want to be famous and *I* want to be admired'? Probably not a lot. But what about somebody who is full of enthusiasm and outlines an idea to you with an emphasis on how many people would benefit from it? Somebody who has genuine concern for others? Such a person is much more likely to attract help than the miserable so-and-so whose exclusive interest is entirely focused on himself.

So, if you try to recruit the help of others, talk to them in an enthusiastic way and with an emphasis on your honest and genuine altruistic motivation. This approach will remove many of the obstacles that you would almost certainly encounter if you were more self-centred. As you can see, the idea of combining your personal wish with an altruistic motivation for others flows like a red thread through every single step of wish-practice and will help you in almost every way.

Exercise
Speed Up Your Progress By Getting Help

Do this once

- Make a list of people who could help you to make your heart-wish come true. This list should include people who could give you tips, people from whom you could learn by example or who could teach you and support you in any other way. You can think of your friends and acquaintances or you can browse the Yellow Pages and the Internet. On your list you could write down:

1. Friends or acquaintances who have already achieved what you want.
2. Counsellors for emotional or relationship-related issues.
3. Workshop teachers, course leaders and any types of other teachers you can think of.
4. Books, books, books.
5. Experts and successful people from whom you can learn by example.
6. Self-help groups.
7. Any kind of meetings where you could encounter like-minded people.

• Approach these people in an appreciative and enthusiastic way and talk to them about your big vision, which includes your genuine altruistic motivation.

If you look for a teacher, mentor or counsellor in your field you don't always need to find experts whose advice costs a lot of money. A friend or acquaintance who can already do what you would like to achieve may serve the purpose just as well. But before you approach someone for help it is a good idea to watch out for two things.

1. The teacher/mentor/experienced friend should make you feel good about yourself and your dreams. You will not gain a lot from a mentor relationship if it weakens your self-esteem and your confidence in your ideas even if your chosen teacher is one of the world's leading experts in her field. You are better off with somebody who is less famous and extraordinary, but who is able to bring out the best in you through helping you to feel good about yourself, your abilities and your wishes.

2. The teacher should be really good himself at what he is teaching. He needs to have integrity and he shouldn't

say one thing but then do another. To put it into the words of the old cliché, a mentor will only be of genuine help to you if he 'walks the talk'. In my work as a psychotherapist I believe that I can only help my clients to reach the same level of contentment and happiness that I have achieved in my own life. I don't think I would go to a parenting counsellor who hasn't got children of her own and therefore hasn't got a real clue what it means to be totally responsible for a baby or a child for twenty-four hours a day. I wouldn't go to a marriage counsellor who has had a string of divorces himself. Equally, I wouldn't listen to a guru who has fine methods but a somewhat fishy character.

The best help you can find is someone from whom you can learn by example. However, this idea is not very popular in our culture because it requires some humility, which some people might mistake for 'humiliation'. In order to learn by example you need to put your own ego on one side for a while, and to tune into the heart-mind of another person in order to adopt parts of it.

Do you remember the house with all your subpersonalities? The ego is the one who considers himself or herself the boss. If you try to learn from other people by example the ego will scream in outrage, 'Don't do this, I am so special, I am sure I can do this *my* way'. The ego protests so strongly because it senses that taking other people as models might seriously undermine its domain of power. It fears (rightly) that we could change so dramatically that it could be made redundant.

But learning by model will never destroy your sense of self; you will simply *transform* in the fastest and easiest way possible. It is this idea that lies behind the guru–disciple relationship in Tibetan Buddhism and I think it is one of its most wonderful gifts. When we as Buddhist students have found a teacher who fits the above requirements, all we have to do is to love our teacher and to open up to him or her and the whole spiritual development of this person will slowly but surely trickle into our heart-mind, making our own development many times faster than if we had to do it all by ourselves. It really resembles a miracle. Everything good I have written in my books, every deeper feeling of true happiness and insight I experience, comes from this slow but wonderful melting-process of my heart-mind with the heart-mind of my teachers.

Learning by model is not limited to spiritual development. You can learn many things in this way. When I was younger I used to live in flats, which I shared with different flatmates. I noticed afterwards that I always learnt something from everybody I lived with in an effortless and unconscious way. For me these were mainly emotional and relationship-related issues. But it might have equally been to learn how to work in an organised and disciplined way or how to become more artistic.

You don't even need to be very close to a person whom you use as your model, although that definitely helps. All you need to do is to genuinely appreciate the positive qualities of this person and to wish to acquire the same abilities as them. Then you need to be patient and to try not to push the process. Learning by model doesn't work through conscious trying but through loving, trusting and letting it happen.

For some people receiving help is quite a challenge. They feel they are failing if they 'have to' visit a self-help group or a counsellor. Frankly, in my eyes, this is rubbish. We never exist for even a second independently from others. We need to buy our food from others, we share living-space, and most of all we need to love and to be loved in order to experience even the most basic happiness. I myself have been in dependent and destructive relationships and I know how awful it is to feel so much at the mercy of other people who don't really care for you. However, the answer is not to attempt to rid yourself of all your neediness. Instead you have to learn to direct your needs to people who don't take advantage of you and who positively support you. Let me put it this way: the more you are able to receive graciously from positive sources and the more you can freely pass on your love and happiness to others, the happier and more emotionally healthy you are.

So, don't block the process of making your dreams come true by stamping your feet like an angry toddler, screaming 'I want to do it on my own!' When you are two years old this is an appropriate attitude. However, if you want to be successful in wish-practice you are better off opening your heart-mind and accepting any form of help that is available for you.

One last word on this issue: sometimes you will find that you approach somebody for help but you don't get a positive response. Don't worry about this because the other person is probably just going through a bad phase, which has nothing to do with you. Remember, difficult people are usually having a difficult time and therefore don't have much to give. Shrug it off and go on finding support somewhere else. In wish-practice you need some persistence and you mustn't be intimidated when you encounter your first setback, or your second or even your twentieth setback.

Be Organised and Intuitive at the Same Time

'Where shall I find the time for all this activity?' I hear you groan.

There is a clear answer to this question.

The only way to gain the time to make your dreams come true is to regard your own wishes as being *as* important as those of others.

I am afraid I don't know of a single exception to this rule. If you regard your needs as more important than those of your friends, colleagues and family members, they will accuse you (rightly) of being egotistical and over time they will withdraw their support.

However, most people in the 'self-development scene' tend to make the other kind of mistake, which is regarding other people's needs as more important than their own. I have a client who is a mother of two small children. She does almost all the housework and childcare, although her partner and father of the children works only part-time. This mother is afraid that she is harming her children if they are in the care of others for too many hours, so she does her work mostly in the evenings and at night, and she looks after her children during the day.

Another woman I know works much longer hours than her husband, organises the entire household and childcare and doesn't object to her husband playing football every Saturday for the whole day.

Both these women complain that they don't have time to pursue their dreams. What can I say? I wouldn't have time if I lived like them. Their lives are the result of years and years of regarding other people's needs as more important than their own and it will not be easy to reverse this process.

I know that it isn't always easy to pursue your own wishes when you have children. Our culture is relentless in judging parents (and particularly mothers) if they don't give the last drop of their life-blood to totally and completely satisfying even the smallest desires of their children. Babies and children would need to be entertained and stimulated every single minute of the day if some guilt-provoking parenting books had their way.

However, I don't see it quite like that. If I look back on my own childhood I remember fondly what my parents did for me. But what I really value are the positive things I learnt from them as models. My mother was and still is an extremely hardworking, utterly disciplined person. Whatever she wanted to achieve she tackled in this way and was promptly successful in no time at all. We are four siblings and I can see her traits in all of us. My father, on the other hand, was more fun-loving, explorative and gentle. I took on all these character traits and these were the real assets I brought from my childhood into my adult life. Whatever other problems I had I used these strengths to solve them, and still do.

What better model can you be for your children than to be a person who genuinely cares for others but also takes the time to make their own dreams come true? Wouldn't that be a worthwhile heritage? Or do you want your children to live the half-suffocated life that you are living at the moment if you continue to regard other people's needs as more important?

Let's go back to the title of this section. Most people I know who pride themselves on being very intuitive are pretty chaotic as well. Their houses looks 'artistically' untidy, they would never even dream of writing a daily work-planner and they are constantly searching for things they have mislaid. On the other hand, most people I know who are very organised and rational don't seem to have much need to be intuitive. They get things done in a systematic and orderly way, which doesn't leave much space to follow their intuitive impulses.

In my opinion both types of people are missing out. Being organised and intuitive at the same time doesn't need to be a contradiction at all. On the contrary, the less time you waste on searching for your keys and working through the jungle of things in your house, the more time and inner space you have to listen to your inner voice of intuition. And the more you can put these impulses into practice in an orderly and systematic way, the quicker you will develop in the field of your choice.

Organising for Intuitive People

Let's first deal with intuitive people who would benefit from being more organised. I will only mention two words that will probably make your toes curl, 'Daily work-planner' and 'to-do list'. I am afraid nobody who wants to be successful in *this* lifetime will get around them. In fact, using these two organising tools will save you a lot of time and, even more important, they will take away the constant pressure and bad conscience of never being really sure that you have caught up with your work. If you have a daily work-planner you only need to do what is written on it for the day and afterwards you can be totally lazy with *a really good conscience*. Wouldn't that be an incentive?

If you have already had a look at some books about getting more organised you perhaps know about the different sorts of to-do lists that are recommended. I think most of them are far too complicated. What you really need is just an A-list and a B-list. The B-list stands for 'All the things I can procrastinate about with a really good conscience' or 'procrastinating list' for short. Here you can list things that you would like to do but it doesn't really matter *when* you do them. For example, if you want to read a certain book that is to do with your dream you can include it here because nothing terrible will happen if you put this off for a few weeks. The A-list stands for 'All the things I am really glad to have done because otherwise I would be in trouble', or 'urgent list' for short. Here you can list things like returning important calls or making a doctor's appointment for your child.

With the help of these two lists you should procrastinate only about those things that you *can* put off and get the really important things done. The result will be that you will feel much more relaxed and much better about yourself. However, you need a daily work planner as well in order to get rid of the stress about the mounting tasks you constantly see all around you.

The best thing to do is to buy a diary that shows one week on one page and has plenty of blank space as well. You can write all the things in it that you have to do and those you really want to do, like that barbecue on Saturday night. In the top right-hand corner you can put your urgent list and in the bottom right-hand corner you can write all the things from your procrastinating list. As the days go by you can try to do *one* thing from your urgent list and only do things from your procrastinating list when you *feel like* doing them.

This doesn't look too awful, does it? If you can follow these simple guidelines you will be astonished at how much you will get done in a week's time, and you will feel even more astonished about how relaxed and free of inner stress you will feel while doing them.

How do you apply all this to making your dream come true?

When you look at your dream and think about all the things you need to do in order to make it come true, you will probably feel either rather overwhelmed by it all or you might get into the mood of rolling up your sleeves and working like a mad person. In either case it is a good idea to first sit down for a while and write an action plan. Brainstorm and write down anything that comes into your mind that needs to be done to make your wish come true. Include all problems that need to be resolved and all obstacles which you need to overcome, even if you haven't the slightest idea how you should do this. And don't forget to add consulting all the people who could help you with your dream. When you have run out of ideas, look at what you have written down and then feel so overwhelmed and discouraged that you screw up your sheet of paper and throw it into the nearest waste-paper basket. Stop, I was only joking!

What you actually do is fit all your work tasks into either of your two to-do lists according to their urgency, or into your diary if you have to keep to deadlines. If you want you can still whinge a bit about all the work and about your fear that you will never be able to solve all these problems. But then you can make yourself a nice cup of tea and relax.

In wish-practice you don't need to know in advance exactly how you want to put everything into practice, and you don't need to do it all yourself, because in one way or the other you will be *guided* to your dream.

Intuition for Rational and Organised People

In addition to doing everything from a more rational and organised point of view you can use your intuition. Your intuition is the voice of your heart and if you have heard it before you know that it is very beautiful and wise. Your intuitive voice has only one disadvantage: it doesn't speak very loudly and it isn't very assertive. As soon as you become very hectic and emotionally dramatic you will not be able to hear it any more.

You can compare your intuition with a computer that works with amazing speed and precision. But if you pour water (emotion) over it, it will quickly be put out of order. So, in order to use your intuition successfully you need to have some basic peace and order in your life, or at least, at times, some quiet and a calm oasis. In other words, if your life is more or less a roller-coaster ride, your intuitive voice can only speak to you when your little train stops to let new passengers in.

Meditation is sometimes recommended as a means of encouraging intuitive insight. In my experience, quiet walks in the countryside or a relaxing cup of tea serve the purpose just as well. You give yourself space, you enjoy being alive and *Voila!* you have a great idea of some kind. That is intuition!

The kind of intuitive insight you receive depends largely on your heart-wish. If you want to be a healer, you will receive guidance to do with healing. If you want to write a book, you will receive ideas to do with your subject. And if you want to buy a house, you might receive an impulse to drive around a neighbourhood you never thought of before. This means that the more you know what you want (Step 1 of wish-practice) and the more you have brought your whole being behind your wish (Step 2) the clearer intuitive guidance you can expect.

Each stage of the wish-practice method (see page 101) is designed to enhance intuitive insight. The relaxation achieved in Stage 1 will help you to connect more and more with the essence of your heart, which is, as you know, the primordial ground itself. From here an abundance of insights and ideas can arise. When you make contact with the divine beings in Stage 2 they can whisper their advice into your heart-mind, and if you are very quiet and relaxed you will be able to hear it. Stages 3 and 4 are creating a feeling-picture in your mind and practising symbol therapy, and they are both excellent tools for developing your intuitive intelligence too.

Simply asking your Higher Consciousness questions without expecting an immediate answer can also be a powerful tool for cranking up your intuition. You will be amazed at how many of your questions will be answered after some time if you write them down in a journal.

Don't expect your intuitive insights to only come to you in the form of your own thoughts and feelings. This will by no means be the case. Your intuitive guidance can equally come to you in the the form of a friend or even a stranger who gives you some advice, or in the form of a book cover that catches your eye as you enter a bookshop. It is important to follow up any of those ideas and tips. Even if they lead to nothing in nine out of ten cases, you will be very grateful when you finally hit the nail on the head.

Intuition is wonderful, but sadly it can't be controlled any more than you can control being happy and enjoying yourself. The harder you try the less it will work. But if you *are* happy you feel it is the most natural thing in the world. It is the same with intuition. Once you hear and feel its voice it feels so natural that you wonder how you could ever have managed without it. But, as with happiness, you can't force it. You need the wish to be happy and intuitive, but be patient at the same time. You need to allow yourself plenty of space for failure without getting annoyed with yourself. And as you become more relaxed and playful you will become happier and more intuitive, and your wish-practice will flower.

BEHAVE AS IF YOU ARE SURE THAT YOUR WISH WILL COME TRUE

This is a very enjoyable step. You need to imagine what you would do if you were absolutely sure that your wish would come true. Let's imagine that your heart-wish is a journey around the world that lasts at least a year. But, so far, you have never travelled more than a hundred miles from your home, you have no money whatsoever to put your dream into reality and your parents would be shocked and angry if they knew what you were planning, and even angrier if you did it.

Working with wish-practice means sticking to your wish despite all these obstacles and despite the fact that you haven't got a clue how to make your dream come true. Now we are going one step further and this means that you have to *behave* as though you are sure that your wish will come true (against all the odds – that is exactly the trick). So, if your wish is a journey around the world, I want you to go out and to buy some small pieces of travel equipment or even a map of a far-flung country. You don't need to spend an awful lot of money on these items. However, it should be enough to tell all your subpersonalities, your divine helpers and most of all yourself that you are very serious about what you want.

A friend of mine wished for a soulmate and I suggested that he went out and bought her a little present or two and wrote her a Valentine's card. Of course he was very reluctant. Doing such things can be a challenge for your ego, which always wants to be in charge. The ego will find it silly to spend money on something that is so uncertain, and if you do it nevertheless it will protest because it will feel that you don't regard it as important enough. And it is absolutely right! If you start acting seriously on your wishes you begin to rely more on your Higher Consciousness, which is much more subtle and less graspable than your big fat ego that always throws a tantrum if it doesn't get its way.

Relying on your Higher Consciousness means doing things that might not always make sense from an ordinary point of view. It means getting more in tune with this huge reservoir of power in yourself that is much more loving and wise than your everyday self.

Even more important than to acquire things is to throw things out. If you want to move have a big clear-out to tell your subconsciousness that you are ready to let go of your old home. If you want better relationships sift through your friends and acquaintances and ask yourself whether it is likely that they will change in ways that are important for you. If not – let them go! If you want a change of career stop doing things like training and having networking meetings with your old colleagues. Instead start to attend meetings in your new field of vocation.

Letting things and people go is always harder than acquiring something new. That is human – we all cling to the security of familiar people and circumstances and we try hard to avoid seeing how detrimental they can be for us and our dreams. However, if you are serious about your wish, start gently letting go, bit by bit, of what is in the way of your desire. Again, do this by consistently making your own needs as important as those of others. Other people often cling to you for their security as much as you might cling to them, and you are not doing them a favour if you blindly submit to them.

However, letting people go doesn't mean being unloving to them or even brutally breaking the contact if they are not in full agreement with your wishes. With family members in particular, many people face the challenge of training in the high art of diplomacy, and of skilfully avoiding any topic that could bring up negative feelings. In that way you can go on pursuing your wishes while still relating to the people who are dear to you but unfortunately not always supportive of your dreams.

One word of warning: don't let other people know about your 'weird' activities of behaving as if you are sure that your wish will come true. What I mean is, don't behave in ways that will upset people around you and don't be phoney. I much prefer being with people who are genuinely and honestly unhappy than with people who are wearing an armour of positiveness that makes any closer contact impossible. If you behave in the way that is described in this section do it privately, and only share it with people who understand and support you.

SEE YOUR ACTIVITIES AS A LEARNING EXPERIENCE

One of the biggest mistakes in wish-practice is thinking that you have to do everything yourself. What follows from this wrong assumption is either resignation or frantic activity that leaves you exhausted and discouraged after only a short while. But if you are not a very trusting and laidback person (like most of us) it can be hard to give up these wrong ideas, in particular when you have worked for quite some time for your wish with no tangible results.

It can be hard to go for another job interview when you have been rejected so many times already. It can be exhausting to go on yet another blind date if you have had no luck so far. You just can't pluck up the hope that it might work this time around; as a result you feel resigned and exhausted, and any more work in order to make your wish come true feels like a terrible chore.

Have courage, help is in sight! There is a remedy for you that will cure your tiredness and hopelessness within one second. Do you know what this remedy is? It's called 're-titling', which means giving something a new title. So far, you have worked under the title 'Making my wish come true', and you might really have had enough of that. So, what about taking action, but now under the heading 'Learning something about myself and my wish'?

For example, if you go on a blind date to find a partner, don't do it solely in order to find somebody, but do it also to learn about other people and about yourself, your wishes and the way you want to relate in a partnership. This will allow you to adjust and refine your wishes in important ways. You might have thought you want such and such a partner, but when confronted with reality you may want to reprioritise your initial wish-list. If you can see your activi-ties of looking for a partner as a learning process, no blind date, no dinner party or whatever will be a waste of time any more because you can always learn something.

You will be astonished at how much energy you suddenly have available through this simple technique of retitling and focusing on what you can learn, rather than solely on the fulfilment of your wish. Retitling is a way of loosening the tight grip of your grasping mind by placing your attention on something else that you consider worthwhile. In that way it is one of the best ways of letting go of too much attachment to your wish.

STEP 3, TAKING ACTION: THE ESSENTIALS

Step 3 of wish-practice tells you how to take skilful, enjoyable action to make your wish come true, employing both your rationality and your intuition. There is only one exercise in this step because the emphasis is on getting up and starting to act in the real world.

- You need to give out what you want to receive in order to obey the law of karma without beating yourself up about it.

- Work for your wish in a way and pace that is enjoyable. Maintaining a good mood in wish-practice is important.

- Overcome your fears and exhaustion by focusing on how you want to contribute to the well-being of others with your wish.

- Give up wrong ideas about independence and search for and accept help in every possible way.

- Work for your wish in an organised way and follow your intuition at the same time.

- Behave as though you are sure your wish will come true (privately, without making anybody wonder whether you have gone mad!).

- Use the technique of 'retitling' to consider your activities not only as way of making your wishes come true, but also as a way of learning about yourself and your desires.

Step 4

Raising Your Vibrations

If you have come so far in wish-practice you are doing really well.

Let's look at what you have done so far. In Step 1 you found your heart-wish and by combining it with an altruistic motivation you also guaranteed that it would make you happy once it was fulfilled. You trained the muscles of your heart-mind by practising the different steps of the wish-practice method in Step 2. Then, in Step 3, you started to work in the outside world for the fulfilment of your wish. What else could you possibly do? Well, there is something called 'raising your vibrations'. Let me explain.

You and your (unfulfilled) wish are not really separate because you both come from the primordial ground from which everything arises. On a deep level we are one with everything, and when we are further on our spiritual path we can experience this more fully through an ever-deepening experience of bliss and clarity that goes beyond everything we know yet. But even now we can experience that the moments of our deepest fulfilment and happiness are those when all sense of separation disappears, for example when we fall in love or in the ecstatic experience of nature and art.

For wish-practice we need to use this insight in order to avoid separating ourselves from our (unfulfilled) wish and in that way creating obstacles that will prevent it from coming true. For example, if you *wish* to be hilariously happy when you have conceived a baby but you *are* continuously depressed and stressed because you haven't conceived yet you have a problem. By being miserable you have separated yourself from the joy you want to feel when your wish is fulfilled. In that way the primordial ground doesn't have so much chance to manifest your wonderful baby because your whole mind is covered and blocked by misery. But the more your mood vibrates on the same wavelength as your wish the more easily it can manifest.

Let me put it a bit more simply: as beans grow best in rich compost, wishes that will make you happy grow best in a happy mind. Makes sense, doesn't it? You still need an egg and a sperm and all that to make a baby, but ultimately it is your heart-mind from which everything will finally come into existence.

Usually we think that if we had this and that it would *make* us happy. However, this is a very superficial view. What really happens is exactly the opposite. We *first* need to experience a positive state of mind and *then* all the wonderful things we wish for can manifest. In other words, we need to be as happy, fulfilled and content *right now* as we wish to be once we have received our heart-wish. Raising your vibration means improving the inner state of your heart-mind to the point where it equals the state of happiness that you are aiming for with your wish. If your heart-mind, which is in essence the primordial ground, can produce these wonderful feelings, it will also be able to bring your correspondent wish into material existence.

'What's the point of wish-practice if I have to become happy all by myself anyway?' you may be complaining.

Wish-practice as it is taught in Buddhism is a spiritual path in its own right. It uses your personal desires, but what it really gives you is a personal development that goes far beyond just getting what you want. Wish-practice teaches you to use your wish-fulfilling gem, but by doing so, you will fall in love with it and you will discover that this gem in itself has everything you have always longed for. The wish-fulfilling gem is your own heart, and by discovering its love and wisdom you can make all your wishes come true and get in addition what no earthly desire will ever provide for you. When you experience the qualities of your heart you will find *unconditional* happiness. Step 4 of wish-practice, 'Raising your vibration', is a first move in this direction.

How can you be happy, even though your wish isn't fulfilled yet?

For some people this question isn't difficult to answer because they have already achieved some basic well-being. But for others it sounds like, 'How can I climb a mountain while standing on only one leg?' or 'How can I eat this gorgeous cake without opening my mouth?'

Maybe you could try to talk yourself into being happy. Maybe you could walk around and tell yourself 500 times a day 'I am really happy and I deserve for my wish to come true.' You tried that already? And it didn't work? OK, scrap this approach then, because I know that it doesn't work. Trying to talk yourself into a better mood is a method that is much too crude and forceful. Nothing will provoke your inner resistance more quickly than the attempt to change yourself by pure force. All your subpersonalities will team up against you in no time if you try to dominate them with affirmations which in their eyes are nothing but silly.

Raising your vibration is not about improving yourself and not about making yourself into a better person. On the contrary, raising your vibration is about becoming more and more yourself in a deeply satisfying sense. Have you still got no idea how to do that?

Well, I'll tell you. The core of any kind of genuine happiness is love. The more you can deeply love something or someone, the higher and happier your vibration will be and the more quickly you can manifest your desire. In a loving and happy state all separation will decrease; you will be more in alignment with the primordial ground and will therefore be able to influence it much more efficiently. And love is the only way to come into closer contact with your Higher Consciousness, which can then assist in bringing your wishes into existence. Raising your vibrations means to awaken the love and the happiness of your heart.

However, it will not be of much benefit if you are just told 'You've *got* to love!' Just *trying* to be kind and loving can easily produce a goody-goody character with all its self-suppression and distortion. What you need is to find a way to *genuinely* link into the love that is waiting for you in your own heart. The next few steps will show you three ways of developing more love and happiness in yourself that really work.

LOVE YOUR WISH ROMANTICALLY AND PASSIONATELY

One of the easiest ways to bring more love into your life is simply to love your wish. If you can love your aim with all your heart you are preparing the best conditions for it to come true. The love and the joy of your heart *are* your wish-fulfilling gem, and the more you are in touch with them the easier it will be for you to influence the primordial ground.

However, it will not be enough if you love and admire your desired aim like an antique statue in a museum. This kind of love is too detached. What we need to raise our vibration successfully is love that creates romantic and passionate attraction, and a lot of it!

Much has been written and said about love and passion, and many people are thoroughly confused about them. So that you can get this point right I want to make it very clear.

The biggest mistake you can make is to confuse romantic passionate love with passionate attachment or obsession. Love and attachment look similar in many ways but they are truly complete opposites. Simply put: love brings happiness and attachment brings suffering.

Romantic and passionate *love* for your wish (good!).	Passionate *attachment* to your wish (bad!).
You find your desired aim wonderful and when you think of it you feel *joy, anticipation and care*.	You find your desired aim wonderful and when you think of it you feel nothing but *greed*.
You feel a great sense of *well-being and genuine happiness* while pursuing your aim.	You feel *painful longing* and *frustrated desire* while pursuing your aim.
You want to have your desired aim but *you care for everybody who is involved* as well.	You want your desired aim so badly that *you pursue it ruthlessly*.
You *focus on the positive contribution* you want to make to the world with your wish.	You just focus on yourself and on your desire and *you don't really care* if anybody benefits from your wish.

Love will help you to make your wishes come true more quickly because it is *the* most positive force in the whole universe. In the light of love:

• The body heals more quickly.

• Pain subsides.

• Children grow into happier and more confident adults.

• Difficult people mellow.

• Plants grow more lush.

• Conflicts are laid to rest.

• Difficult emotions are easily overcome.

• Your intuition improves amazingly.

• *Wishes come true more quickly*.

If you learn to give your heart and its qualities of love, joy, compassion and heartfelt wisdom more importance in your life you will improve every aspect of it. Not only will you feel wonderful, but you will also strengthen your immune system and your relationships; you will become more compassionate; and you will experience much less stress. Even your intuition and intelligence will improve, and you will be able to resolve any of your problems much more easily. And best of all, your wishes will come true much more quickly – naturally and effortlessly.

It is one of the biggest misunderstandings of humankind to believe that it can be dangerous to open your heart. People are afraid that they could be invaded or harmed by the negative energy of those around them. This is completely untrue – nobody and nothing can harm you when you open your heart, and experience the love and the wisdom that comes from it. On the contrary, an open and loving heart is the best psychic protection there is. The worst that can happen is that your love is rejected. Yes, I know that can hurt a bit; I have experienced it myself. But to close your heart and to cut yourself off from your own flow of love and wisdom hurts a thousand times more. I have experienced that, too.

If there was an exam to be passed in wish-practice, it would be the amount of love you can give to your wishes and to the people you want to benefit from them that would determine how many points you achieved. The most advanced practitioners of wish-practice can virtually 'love their wishes into existence'. They feel themselves pulled towards whatever they desire by a string that is fixated in their heart. It is the pull on their heart that will finally lead them with unwavering intuition to the fulfilment of their wish.

I wish I could claim that I am such a perfect practitioner of wish-practice. I have to admit that I am often still quite far away from this ideal. However, I seem to be able to make

quite a few of my wishes come true, and you also don't need
to worry if you are not perfect yet. The primordial ground is
not so strict. Even if we do half the required things wrong it
still gives us what we want.

USE YOUR WISHES TO DEVELOP MORE LOVE

One of the best way to raise your vibration and to find love
and happiness in yourself is to wish for others the same
amount of happiness, love and fulfilment that you wish for
yourself. If you can do this whole-heartedly it can change
your entire emotional landscape from a miserable, rainy day
into beautiful sunshine in a very short time.

Exercise
Raise Your Vibration

*Do this as often as you like and whenever you feel the need to
raise your vibration*

• Remember the part of your wish-list that describes how
  you want to feel, once your wish is fulfilled. For example,
  if you wish to have a baby you probably want to feel a
  deep feeling of bonding and caring. You want to love
  from all your heart and deeply enjoy your cuddly little
  baby.

• Now, instead of wishing to have these feelings only for
  yourself and for your family, wish that *everybody* in the
  whole world could experience feelings of bonding,
  caring, love and joy. Of course, not everybody wants a
  baby, but every single person in the world wants to
  experience these kinds of feelings. On this level all
  human beings are totally the same. If you want success in
  business, wish for all beings to feel joyful, energetic and

empowered, or whatever else you want to feel. Again, on a level of feeling everybody wants to have these kinds of emotions, no matter whether they want to have a business or not.

- Make it a habit to always send out these kinds of good wishes to all beings in the world (including yourself), whenever your wish comes to mind. You will be astonished at how much happiness, contentment and inner calm this will bring to you. When your positive feelings become more stable your wish can manifest.

Don't underestimate the strength of this exercise. The more you can work with it in a relaxed and joyful way, the more empowered and satisfied you will feel. You can practise it whenever your wish comes to mind and when you don't need to concentrate fully on what you are doing at that moment. Don't force these thoughts; instead try to link into your intuitive understanding that *really* all people want to experience the same kind of positive feelings that you want for yourself.

The good news is that there is no shortage of happy and fulfilled feelings in this world – you can be totally generous with them. And the better everybody feels the more energy and motivation they will have to pass this happiness on to others. It is a self-perpetuating process that will create more and more fulfilment and happiness, the more people join in.

When a friend of mine wished to buy a flat it looked at some point as if everything in the universe had conspired *against* her and it started to get her down. But every time she could focus her thoughts on good wishes for others she felt so much better. When the negative feelings about the flat and all the obstacles she experienced came up she repeated several times in her mind, 'May all people have a place where they feel really at home. May all people have a home that is a peaceful haven and helps them to relax.' Saying this, she could feel that she wasn't alone in her wish for such a home and that in fact we all long for a place like this. This realisation was enough to take away most of her frustration and to rebuild her trust that everything would work out fine in the end (which it did only shortly afterwards).

The practice of raising your vibration is the informal part of the wish-practice method and you can do it as much as you like, as long as you feel good about it. The aim of this exercise is to make you *feel better*, so that you become ready to receive your wish.

MAKE AN OFFER TO THE UNIVERSE

In this section we will go even one step further in focusing on what we have to give, rather than on what we want to have. We will do this in the form of making an offer to the universe, which means that we will make a declaration about what we have to offer in exchange for what we want. Doing this will have several benefits:

- Making an offer to the universe will make you more confident. Focusing on giving will make you aware of how much you possess, rather than how much you lack, and coming into contact with your inner richness is one of the best confidence boosters you can think of.

- Making an offer to the universe will strengthen your trust that you truly deserve what you want. Deep in your unconscious mind you *know* that you can only get what you are willing to give because this is how the universe works. By making an offer you are obeying the law of karma, which rules the world.

- Making an offer to the universe will bring you into contact with your inner love. It will raise your vibrations, and in that way your wish can manifest much more easily.

I suggest that you jump in straight away and start to draw up a list of things, attitudes and emotions you have to offer in the area of your wish. You have already formulated on your wish-list how you want to contribute to the world once your wish is fulfilled. Now you can add what you have to offer to the people from whom you expect the fulfilment of your wish. For example, if you wish for a soulmate you need to write down everything that you have to offer to your future partner. That includes everything from the emotional and sexual level, but also everything you have to offer in the area of finances and commitment. Be honest: don't write anything down that you don't really want to share. If you don't want to marry or share your finances, stand by it – you don't have to. (However, in this case don't expect a partner who would want to share everything she or he has, either.)

On the other hand, don't hide your light under a bushel. You probably have more to offer than you think – everything counts. For example, if you want a certain job you might not have all the required qualifications, but you might be committed, enthusiastic and a really humorous person. I certainly would want such a colleague. On your list of offers you can add things like having a positive motivation (huge asset) and having a good heart (best asset of all). You can include abilities like homemaking and listening and your *desire* to pay even if you have no idea where you should get the money from.

It is a scientifically proven fact that women habitually underestimate their qualities and that men do the opposite. Sociologists have found this out by researching the different ways in which both sexes apply for jobs, as well as how they advertise in lonely hearts' columns. So, as a rule of thumb, if you are a typical woman add 25 per cent of whatever you have to offer to your list, and if you are a typical man subtract 25 per cent. I am sorry if I have now offended a few sensitive men. In either case it can be a good idea to consult a trustworthy friend to get feedback about what you have to offer. In many cases you will find that you have much more to give than you thought.

Once you have written your list you need to compare it with your initial wish-list. If you see a great disparity between your two lists you might need to make some adjustments. Remember, despite the fact that you can create whatever you want from the primordial ground, you have to obey the law of karma as well and that means that you have to give what you want to have.

If you are an eighty-year-old man and you want to have a gorgeous twenty-year-old girlfriend but you don't want her to inherit a penny of your enormous wealth you will have a problem. Or if you want to be a great musician but you don't offer time, discipline and dedication to learn your instrument something is wrong as well. In both cases you are not obeying the law of karma. Equally, if you are a capable woman and you don't dare to go for the full monty in your career you are not using all your potential. Go on, shoot for the moon! All you need is the honest *intention* to give the best you have in return.

Exercise
Make an Offer to the Universe

*Do this once

- Write a list of everything that you have to offer in the area of your wish. Include your abilities and your finances, but also your attitudes, emotions and intentions (for example your intention to pay for what you wish for, even if you have no money yet). Now compare this list with your initial wish-list and decide if your offer matches your desire. If it does, fine; if it doesn't, try to adjust your offer or your wish until you get a roughly even match.

- Plan for a special time and place to make your offer to the universe. If you like you can include some incense, ritual and prayer as well.

- When the time has arrived, read out your offer to the universe with passion and dedication. Then add, 'I invite all people who like my offer and who would be able to fulfil my wish to come to me for the best of all beings.'

- Keep the list of your offer in a special place and read through it from time to time.

For many people it feels deeply empowering to send out not only wishes but offers as well. Think about anybody who is very successful and genuinely happy. No matter what field these people excel in, they usually have one thing in common: they all have a lot to offer to other people.

STEP 4, RAISING YOUR VIBRATIONS: THE ESSENTIALS

Step 4 is a short one, but it is nevertheless very important. It can be summarised in one sentence, 'As beans grow best in rich compost, wishes that will make you happy grow best in a happy mind.'

- Raising your vibrations means becoming as happy *now* as you want to be once your wish is fulfilled.

- The core of genuine happiness is love and opening your heart is the doorway to your Higher Consciousness and will make it easier to influence the primordial ground.

- You can start by loving your wish romantically and passionately, but please don't confuse passionate love with passionate attachment.

- Think of how you want to feel once your wish is fulfilled. Wish for all beings in the universe to feel these wonderful feelings as well. Do this as often as you like and every time your wish comes to mind.

- Draw up a list of all the things, attitudes, feelings and intentions you have to offer in the area of your wish. Make an offer to the universe and invite all people to you who like your offer and who can give you what you wish for.

Step 5

Overcoming Your Craving

In Steps 1 to 4 of wish-practice you basically learnt every-thing that you need to do in order to make your wishes come true. Find your heart-wish, use the power of your heart-mind, work for your wish and raise your vibrations. That's all – only four steps!

What are the other four steps for? Well, the next four steps will tell you what you *shouldn't* do in order not to mess up the beautiful process of letting things arise from the primordial ground according to your liking. There are so many pitfalls and traps you can encounter that they need four more steps so that you can recognise them and avoid them successfully.

THE EVIL OF CRAVING AND ATTACHMENT

The greatest 'evil' in wish-practice is craving and attach-ment. Whenever you have a wish and you grow impatient and frustrated because it hasn't come true after two days, you are at risk of spoiling the process of wish-practice. This is a pretty big risk, I admit, because it is very difficult to be totally serene and detached when you have first been encouraged to have 'unrealistically' high wishes and to love them passionately and romantically. 'Wish-practice,' you might complain, 'demands impossible things.'

But before you get discouraged, let me tell you one thing: You are even more at risk of experiencing craving and frustration if you are *not* working with wish-practice. If you don't work with your wishes consciously it doesn't mean that you have no unfulfilled desires. On the contrary your desires are still in your mind – but because you are trying to ignore them you will experience them just as inner tensions. These unrecognised longings will create a lot of frustrated craving and, even worse, you might be trying to deaden these feelings with too much alcohol, too much eating or through depression. It is *much* easier to acknowledge your wishes and to learn to deal with any negative feeling you might experience around them.

If you work with wish-practice you will (almost definitely) encounter some craving, but it will be clear and out in the open and therefore you can deal with it skilfully. In other words, the process of overcoming your attachment is part of wish-practice and as you learn to do that you will become happier in every part of your life. If you try to suppress your wishes your craving will come out in neurotic and addictive symptoms, and it will take an awful lot of work to deal with them. (And your wishes will still not be fulfilled.)

How do you know that you are experiencing attachment and craving? That's easy to answer.

If you use your wish-fulfilling gem by rattling it, squeezing it or shouting at it you have become too greedy and your gem will stubbornly refuse to give you what you desire. On the other hand, if you ignore your jewel or if you sulk at it from a distance you are not doing much better because your gem will only work if you can hold it in the highest and most appreciative regard.

Craving is basically every bad feeling you experience

around your wish: greed, unfulfilled painful longing, impatience, frustration, anger, constant worrying, hopelessness, depression, despair, obsessive thinking, feelings of being possessed and so on.

Only if you feel positive about your wish and if you are able to look forward to its fulfilment without any negative feelings or thoughts tainting your experience do you understand that you have successfully avoided the pitfall of craving.

It is almost impossible to avoid any of the above negative feelings when you embark on a wish that you want really badly. For a long time it was a complete mystery to me how you could get rid of them. When I was single I longed for a partner like a shipwrecked person longs for a lifeboat (at least in the beginning).

Many times I got the sympathetic advice 'to let go' more, which drove me totally mad. 'How can I let go of something that I want so badly,' I raged, and demanded further explanations. But my well-meaning friends couldn't explain it to me; they just knew that I was blocking the process through my extreme desire. I got this advice from at least ten different people (including Buddhist teachers), and each time it made me more angry and confused. But then I slowly began to understand.

I knew that one of the most important teachings of the Buddha says that craving is the root of all suffering and that you have to let it go in order to experience even the most basic happiness. It dawned on me that the Buddha didn't say 'let go of your wishes' – on the contrary, making wishes is an encouraged and valuable practice in Tibetan Buddhism. So, it wasn't the wishes that were the problem, it was only the craving – the negative feelings of greed, impatience and frustration – which often goes along with the wishes. This insight gave me a lot of relief. At least I didn't have to let go of my wish for a partner – I just had to figure out how to get rid of my negative feelings around my wish.

The same is true for you. If I say overcome your craving for your wish, it doesn't mean let go of your wish. It means to work for your wish as passionately as before but to let go of the negative impatient feelings you might feel around it. Letting go of craving does *not* mean becoming a bloodless person without passion for life. This is shown in the following diagram.

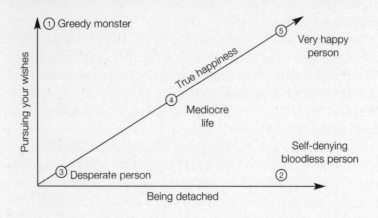

This diagram tells you that you will become like a greedy monster (1) if you pursue your wishes in a totally attached and greedy way, and that you will become a self-denying, bloodless person (2), when you are completely detached and self-denying at the same time. (This is *not* the position of an ascetic because such a person *desires* to live like that and is therefore pursuing his or her wishes.)

The worst position you could be in is when you experience strong cravings while denying yourself all your wishes, and you would probably be pretty desperate there (3). Living a mediocre life means allowing yourself a few wishes while having some cravings as well (4). This is probably what most people do. However, the happiest position is the one where you pursue all your wishes while being totally free of craving at the same time – a very happy person who is developing fast (5).

How can you pursue your wishes passionately while being simultaneously detached? How can you invest your deepest heart-feelings into your desire while completely letting go of control and attachment?

To answer these questions you need to understand that there are two phases in wish-practice, which are called the yang (= activity) phase and yin (= letting go) phase. The yang phase is the time when you actively work for your wish, whereas in the yin phase you step back and let things happen without interfering any more. If you look closely you can find a multitude of processes that function exactly according to this pattern. The following list will show you a few examples of the dynamic of the yang and yin phases in wish-practice.

Wish	Yang phase	Yin phase	Likely result
Going to sleep.	Get ready for bed.	Stop trying to force sleep.	Sleep.
Remembering a name.	Search your memory.	Stop trying.	You remember.
Growing flowers.	Sow the seeds.	Don't dig them up.	Flowers grow.
Making friends.	Show interest, invite.	Don't ring every day.	Interest comes back.
Fulfil your heart-wish.	Work for your wish.	Let go of your craving.	Your wish will be wish fulfilled.

You can find the pattern of a yang and yin phase every time you want to make a wish come true. You always have to do something in the beginning to set up the conditions. However, if you do too much after that you will spoil the process. For example, the more you 'try' actively to fall asleep the less you will succeed in doing so. The more often you ring someone you like the more likely it is that you will get on their nerves. And the more you try to force the process of wish-practice the less you will achieve.

But if you don't do anything at all, nothing will happen

either. If you want to be successful in making your wishes come true, you need to learn the high art of knowing how much to do and when to stop interfering any more. In other words, skilful wish-practice depends on the proper harmony of the yang and the yin phases, and increases the likelihood that you can ask things into existence. Ultimately, the process of wish-practice is a mystery, and it would be a big mistake to think you are completely in control. It is exactly this control that you need to surrender in the yin phase and that can be very difficult when you have already worked very hard for your wish.

When Nigel and I wanted to buy a new house I had a very interesting conversation with my estate agent Peter about this very dynamic. Peter has his feet firmly on the ground and I doubt that he had ever heard of wish-practice. But in his business of selling houses he deals with making wishes come true all the time. He said to me that nine out of ten sales go through exactly at the moment when people start to give up hope. Over the years he had noticed that people first put a lot of time and energy into selling and buying a house, often without results. But then they get tired and a bit resigned and they might book a holiday; that is exactly the moment, Peter said, when it all happens. You have probably heard similar stories as well, for example about couples who conceived a baby exactly at the moment when they had given up hope.

When you do wish-practice skilfully you don't need to come to the point when you lose hope and start to give up in order to enter the yin phase. Instead you can learn to experience it with joy.

How can you do that?

The first thing is to let go of the assumption that the universe owes you something and that because it doesn't deliver you have a perfect right to stamp your foot and howl in frustration. The universe doesn't work like that. It doesn't owe us a nice childhood or a nice partner, nor does it owe us money or health. Even if you are the only person in the whole world who is poor, ill and unhappy it is you and only you who can sow the seeds for change and attract the help to get out of this misery. But if you keep being sulky about 'the unfairness' of it all, you will not be able to do wish-practice properly and will invariably end up with a lot of frustration and craving.

But once you realise that you are in charge of your life you are on the right track. Then you are ready to let go of the next wrong attitude, and that is trying to control *when* your wish should be fulfilled. You are not the only person who wants 'it' now – we all do. However, we need to grow up a little bit from this greedy toddler attitude and accept that every wish has its own time-scale to come into existence as much as every seed has its own time-scale to grow into a mature plant. As big plants take longer to grow, big wishes often take longer as well and there is nothing you can do to speed up the process.

When you have accepted that the universe doesn't owe you anything and that you can't control the speed at which your dream will come true you are ready to work whole-heartedly on the first four steps of wish-practice, which is the yang phase, and you are now ready to enter the yin phase of letting go of control and craving. That means you have to let go of your constant obsessing about your wish so that your heart-mind can do the work that is needed without you interfering the whole time.

How do you let go of your thoughts and feelings around your wish without suppressing them? How do you let go of your obsessing without upsetting any of your subpersonalities? How do you manage finally to go to sleep on a sleepless night?

It won't work if you just *try not* to think, worry and obsess about your object of desire. That would be like saying: 'Try not to think about the heavenly blue hippopotamus under your kitchen table!' The harder you try not to think about it the more the sweet hippopotamus will appear in your mind. The same is true if you just *try* not to worry about your wish – you will find that you think about your wish even more.

What you really need is a change of focus for your mind. You need to find a substitute for your attention that is so interesting and so much fun that it will successfully distract you, while not preventing your wish from coming true.

For example, if you are obsessing about getting a boyfriend and you realise that this doesn't make you more attractive to a potential partner, don't just *try* to stop craving. It won't work. Instead find something to focus your mind on as a substitute. Television and similar distractions will probably not do if your greed and desire are very strong. Your mind needs something really positive to hold on to in order to forget your wish for a while and not to brood over it like a hen over her egg.

I will tell you first the best way to overcome your craving and later on I will give you a few more alternatives that also work very well. You can choose the way that suits you and your temperament best, and you will know that you have been successful in letting go of your attachment when you feel completely positive about your wish.

The ultimate way of overcoming your craving is to concentrate on your positive wishes for others.

When you think of your big vision of how others will benefit from your own wish you will be able to let go of your self-absorption and your craving; you will become happier and in that way your wish can manifest.

But don't forget, overcoming your cravings doesn't mean that you should forget your wish altogether. On the contrary, you need to keep your wishes while trying to let go of your control at the same time. The best way to do this is make your wish in a very concentrated way, and then relax and think about something completely different. This is why you should work with the wish-practice method only once or twice a day and not more. If you tried to visualise your wish continuously, you would almost certainly end up in a too controlling frame of mind.

**This is the way it works: make your wish – and then relax
and think about something different ... work for your
wish – and then relax and do something else ...**

However, if you have to do *a lot* of work in order to make
your wish come true, you face the challenge of bringing the
yang and yin phase together into one harmonious move-
ment. You need to do everything that is necessary to make
your wish come true (yang) and be detached and free of
craving at the same time (yin).

That sounds more difficult than it is, but you can achieve
it by making sure that you *enjoy* working for your wish. If
you have forgotten how you can work for your wish in an
enjoyable way go back to Step 3. Basically it is the same old
story of focusing on your contribution to the world rather
than merely on yourself. By working in a light-hearted and
enjoyable way, you will be able to create enough space to
enable the yin phase of wish-practice to take place even while
you are in the midst of a lot of work for your wish.

One of my biggest successes in wish-practice took place
when I managed (without realising it) to be completely free
of craving. At that point I lived in one bedroom in a shared
flat, and I worked as a social worker, which I found to be a
pretty stressful job. When I visualised my future husband
(with quite a bit of craving, I admit) I also visualised that we
would live in a beautiful house together.

The house wasn't really so important to me; it just served
as a kind of background scenery for my perfect relationship,
which is why I didn't crave for it. It had a white-tiled balcony
with a white railing overlooking a park with dark green
conifers, a beautiful lake and gentle hills in the distance. For
me that was the most desirable place I could imagine. There
was plenty of space in the house, the colours were mostly
white and cream, and I saw myself living there in a very
meditative way. I had just a few clients and I tended my
beautiful garden. My husband was a business consultant

(don't ask me why) and we had the perfect relationship in a perfect house. This place was heaven compared with the way I lived at the time and it honestly didn't occur to me that I could *really* get it.

I had this fantasy every night for several years and then I met Nigel, a business consultant (!), and we fell in love with each other at first sight. Shortly afterwards he set out to find a house for us to live in and made an offer on one he found very exciting (he didn't know about my fantasy). The next time I visited him he took me to see the house and I got a shock. It was the house of my secret dreams!

There was the white-tiled balcony with a white banister overlooking a park with dark green conifers. Beyond the park was the beautiful lake and the hills in the distance, exactly how I had imagined them. The house was white, and had lots of space and a big garden I could tend. It had big windows and light carpets – everything exactly as in my 'fantasy'. I told Nigel how I had visualised this house for years and we were both quite dumbstruck. I really had believed in wish-practice – kind of. But this house was more than I had expected.

USE SYMBOL THERAPY TO OVERCOME YOUR CRAVING

Attachment and craving are so detrimental to wish-practice that you need to do everything you can to let them go. I have strong desires and passions and I know how difficult, if not impossible, it is to become totally light-hearted, trusting and heavenly serene. It is so much easier to stamp your foot and scream words of abuse. The good news is that you don't have to overcome your cravings completely. Even if you, like myself, maintain a few of your old attachments, your wishes can still manifest.

But if you are so attached to your wish that you feel it

would be a complete disaster if it didn't come true you have a problem and you will need to do something about it.

You have to find a way to feel that it would be 'great' if your wish comes true and that it would be at least 'OK' if it doesn't. Imagine how your life would develop if your wish stayed unfulfilled and try to make your peace with that.

If you can't do this you will put your wish-practice under a lot of unnecessary strain and the primordial ground doesn't work very well under pressure (nobody does!).

One of the most effective ways to overcome your negative attachment is to practise symbol therapy for wish-practice. My clients have used symbol therapy to overcome their cravings with great success. As with your first healing symbol (see Step 2), this method will help you to let go of any negative feelings. How it does that has remained a mystery. Symbol therapy has helped many people and you can use it too in order to get over the highest hurdles of wish-practice. There is only one little catch – you have to do it. Symbol therapy won't help you if you just read about it, you need to give it a try. Here is how:

Exercise
Symbol Therapy for Overcoming Your Craving and Negative Attachment to Your Wish

*Do Part 1 once
*Do Part 2 for two minutes on a daily basis as part of the wish-practice method and every time you start obsessing again

Part 1

Preparation:

• Measure on a scale from zero to ten how much craving

you experience (zero is totally happy and serene and ten is feeling mad with frustration and greed).

- Relax in a way that is convenient to you. (You can use the relaxation at the beginning of the 'World of happiness' exercise on page 48 if you like.)

In deep relaxation:

- You are now ready to come into contact with your Higher Consciousness, who will help you to overcome all your attachment. See your Higher Consciousness as an angelic being or as a beautiful shimmering light that has a living and loving quality. Feel how you are embraced by the love and support of your Higher Consciousness.

- Ask your Higher Consciousness, 'Can you please give me a healing-symbol to overcome my suffering, which comes from craving for my wish, for the best of all beings.'

- You might be shown one or several symbols (for example flowers, gems, geometrical forms) and you should pick one that you find attractive and that has a beautiful and bright colour. Acknowledge the very first thought or idea of a symbol that comes into your mind. If you are not sure whether you have received the right symbol you can check with your Higher Consciousness. Watch for an inner feeling of 'yes' or 'no'.

- When you have received a healing symbol you feel good about thanking your Higher Consciousness for its help.

- Say to yourself, 'I always love myself deeply with all my weaknesses and even if I still crave for my wish.'

- Visualise your healing-symbol in the middle of your chest in your heart, and when you breathe out, exhale the colour of your symbol throughout your body, into the surroundings of your body and into your world.

When you breathe in, just enjoy the presence of your symbol in your heart. Then exhale the colour and the positive qualities of your symbol again. Do this *in a loving way* for two minutes. Then open your eyes again.

Part 2

Daily practice:

- Visualise or feel your healing-symbol in your heart whenever you start to crave and for two minutes a day in a loving way on a regular basis as part of the wish-practice method. If you want you can alternate practising this healing-symbol with your previous one from Step 2. Always start by saying, 'I always love myself deeply with all my weaknesses and even if I still crave a lot for my wish.' Visualise your symbol in *exactly* the form it was given to you by your Higher Consciousness and never change it yourself. If it seems to change of its own accord, don't allow this to happen, but always go back to its original form.

- After two weeks measure on your scale how much your craving has diminished. You can expect to be at least two points down the scale. You don't need to be zero on the scale in order to be successful with wish-practice. If you are four or less you should be all right.

SURRENDER CONTROL TO YOUR HIGHER CONSCIOUSNESS

If you have a strong trust and belief in your Higher Consciousness – now is the time for prayer. You need to pray for help to make your wish come true and then you let go. Every mature spiritual person knows that it is no good trying to order their Higher Power around when you pray to him or her; instead you need humility and surrender. In the yin phase of wish-practice you can hand your wish over to your Higher Consciousness and surrender all control.

But please remember that your Higher Consciousness can't make your wishes come true altogether. If it could people wouldn't need to write volumes and volumes on how to manifest your heart's desire. Instead we would all simply pray and receive whatever we want.

The Higher Powers of the universe can only *assist* us in our own effort and help things to go more smoothly. And they can only do so if we try to come more in alignment with them. The more we concentrate on our altruistic motivation and the more we try to incorporate genuine love into our personal wishes, the closer we come to our Higher Consciousness and the more help we can expect.

Many people believe that they are surrounded by angels and guides. In Buddhism we believe that in the head of a needle you can find more enlightened beings than there are grains of sand on all the beaches of the Earth together. If we could only wake up to this truth, letting go of control wouldn't be so difficult. If we could realise that we could be guided by Higher Powers in every step we take, it would be much easier to open up to this help.

The guidance of your Higher Consciousness will come to you in subtle ways. It is not likely that one day an angel will knock on your door and hand over to you the complete instructions for how to find your desired aim, including a bottle of delicious-tasting self-confidence enhancer. Instead divine guidance will come to you through ideas, impulses and feelings that feel more or less just like your own. But these impulses are put into your consciousness by the Higher Powers you have asked for help. They are moments of sudden clarity, of increased courage and deep love.

Equally you might be sent a friend or a book that will help you in important ways. If you don't expect to be helped in these ways you can easily dismiss these fleeting moments;

later on you'll wonder why you never receive any help and why your intuition continues to fail you.

But you can trust that you are helped. The very fact that you have the ability to love is your connection to your Higher Consciousness. If you allow yourself to feel the vulnerability of your heart your Higher Consciousness can help you, remove obstacles for you and give you intuitive guidance. This is the yin phase of wish-practice – enjoy it!

FOCUS ON HAVING FUN

Let me repeat. In order to prise your mind successfully away from your constant craving and worrying around your wish you need a strong and attractive replacement focus. In my experience having fun is an excellent way of achieving this distraction. Don't pursue your wishes in a bitterly serious fashion. Seriousness is the precursor of rigidity and then nothing can move. Instead pursue wish-practice like a great game that is really fun to play.

Do you remember when you built a sand castle as a child? Or when you made things with paper and glue? That was fun, wasn't it? Wish-practice is the most creative game of them all. The frame of mind you had as a child when you were playing happily and unconcernedly is the best frame of mind you can have to make your dreams come true.

Unfortunately, not everybody is able to play as happily as an unconcerned child. But what you *can* do is to focus on the bits of wish-practice that are fun. For example, even if you don't like doing presentations for your work you might enjoy wearing smart clothes. So you could concentrate on the pleasure of that. Focus on flirting with people and having fun with them instead of seriously searching for a partner. (You will be so much more attractive like that as well!)

Imagine you are the star of your own sitcom with an invisible audience that laughs about the way you pant and

scramble after your desires. Wouldn't it be a relief to be able
to join in? Self-deprecating humour can actually be learnt.
You just need to allow yourself to exaggerate a little and to
become a little over-the-top in order to see the funny side of
things.

I learnt this from my first Buddhist teacher, Wilhelm, who
never allowed his students to talk about their problems in a
serious way. When we wanted to tell him about our problems we had to take a guitar and sing them to him! Imagine
that. At that point in my life I still frequently felt quite
desperate. I was so lonely, I was so afraid and I had very
little hope that things could get better. And I had to sing
about it and make a tragic-comedy out of it!

But this method worked like a miracle drug. After I had got
over my first resistance to ridiculing the suffering that felt so
real to me, I started to take it less and less seriously. More and
more often, in the middle of the tears, I burst out laughing. I
just couldn't buy into this tragic show any more. Not long
afterwards my attacks of desperation stopped altogether.

If you now say you can't do this because your own suffering is worse than mine, I disagree. When we suffer it always
feels terrible, no matter whether someone else has even
more problems. So, if I could develop some humour in the
midst of suffering, you can as well.

BE GRATEFUL

'More advice from pious auntie Mary,' I hear you groan.

Wait a minute, auntie Mary is not altogether stupid. She
does have some grains of wisdom and to be grateful is one.
She probably calls it 'Count your blessings' or 'Every cloud
has a silver lining'.

Let me repeat another time. You need to find a way to stop
obsessing about your unfulfilled wish and to stop poisoning
your mind with your craving. Only then can the miracle of

things popping into existence from 'nowhere' happen. So, in order to stop being taken over by your attachment you can focus on your offer, on having fun, or you can practise prayer and symbol therapy. If any of that works for you – fine. But if you are still full of negative feelings around your unfulfilled wish you should try the gratefulness exercise.

The gratefulness exercise was the turning point in my life. It helped me more than anything else to take my mind away from my inner and outer negativity and direct it to something I felt genuinely positive about. And it is such a simple practice that it hardly deserves the title 'exercise'. But for the sake of clarity I present it here as an exercise.

Exercise
The Gratefulness Exercise

***Do this daily if you experience a lot of craving**

- Say to yourself, 'I am grateful for . . .' and then add the first thing that comes to your mind. This doesn't need to be something positive; you can equally add something you feel bad about. (For example 'I am grateful that my partner was so awful to me yesterday . . .')

- Then finish your sentence with '. . . because . . .' and add a genuine reason why you are grateful. (For example, 'I am grateful that my partner was so awful to me yesterday because it forces me to make a decision about whether we should stay together.')

- Go on in this fashion for five to ten minutes. Repeat over and over, 'I am grateful for . . .', and add the first thought that comes to your mind, no matter whether it is positive or negative, and find a genuine reason for your gratefulness.

- Do this exercise frequently until it becomes second nature.

That's all. I told you, it's very simple. I did this exercise for several years with my morning tooth-brushing routine because I always felt worst when I had just woken up. As a result I usually turned up at work in a pretty good mood. After all, there was nothing left in my life I could grumble about. I was grateful for *everything*! This exercise only feels contrived when you start doing it. Once you are in the swing of it you will quickly realise that there is indeed something to be genuinely grateful about in everything.

Even if you had an awful childhood with abuse and neglect, remember that your parents have given you the biggest gift of all – they have given you life! As a human being you can use the power of your mind and create a future that is a thousand times better than your terrible childhood. And through your suffering and the wounds your parents inflicted on you, you are probably much more compassionate and able to help others than the average person. Even if the worst of the worst happened to you there is always a lesson to be learnt that can make you into a more mature being. That is something worthwhile you can be grateful for.

One of the happiest people I know is my friend Jutta. She is very interesting, because from an ordinary point of view she has lost most things that are important to many people. She had a business with her husband that went bankrupt twice. She is separated from her husband and she is now alone at the age of fifty. She lost her house and her two boys have flown the nest. She tries to survive doing part-time jobs with a minimum of money and her childhood was nothing less than awful. But nobody could be happier than her.

What Jutta *has got* is an unwavering motivation to develop in such a way that she can be of real benefit to all beings. She has a Buddhist teacher who guides her on her way and the potential of her heart-mind is unfolding beautifully. Jutta has always been a great inspiration to me because she knows how to turn the negative things in life into something you can be deeply grateful for.

LEARN ABOUT YOUR CURRENT SITUATION

Another way of appreciating your current state before your wishes are fulfilled and of letting go of your constant craving is to focus on what you can learn from it.

There is a saying that goes something like this: 'Life is hard but once you have accepted this it isn't hard any more'.

What does that mean?

A lot of suffering comes from the expectation that everything in people's lives should go smoothly and pleasantly. When I was a child I thought that I would always be happy once I was finally grown up. However, when I was an adult I had even more problems than I had as a child and teenager, and I was horrified. Being a grown-up was not at all as nice as I had expected and I felt betrayed, angry and finally depressed. These feelings added an enormous amount of suffering to my already existing problems and made it even more difficult to solve them.

Then I encountered Buddhism and learnt the first noble truth of the Buddha, which says, freely translated, 'life is full of suffering'. In the second noble truth the Buddha explains that the human world is full of preprogrammed frustrations because we always look for happiness in the wrong places and because nothing can satisfy us for long.

Learning about these truths relieved me to some extent because I realised that there was nothing wrong with me and my suffering. On the contrary, the Buddha said that suffering was the normal state of the average human. However, there was light at the end of the tunnel because the third and the fourth noble truths state that there is a way to end the suffering through the application of ethical living, meditation and the awakening of the loving heart.

When these teachings slowly trickled into my mind a shift in my attitude to the world took place. Instead of being angry and full of self-pity, I saw my life with all its problems as a big classroom in the school for love and happiness. Problems were no longer a nuisance and also started to be the daily bread of my schoolwork, which I could accept much more happily. And the way to pass my exams was to develop more equanimity, love, compassion and happiness. For me it is definitely true that life isn't very hard any more since I have accepted that it *is* hard. The way I did that was to 'retitle' my problems into learning challenges and to tackle them one by one without drowning in self-pity or rage.

If you see the time of your unfulfilled wish as nothing else but a nuisance you block the process of making your wishes come true and you miss out on a great opportunity to learn about unconditioned happiness. The times in our lives when we *don't* have what we want are actually the most precious because then we are forced to find in our own hearts the fulfilment and the happiness that is not dependent on outer conditions any more.

When we are lonely, poor, ill and unfulfilled we can learn to find in the depth of our heart-minds a happiness that is totally independent of our outer conditions. (We can, of course, learn all these things in times when our lives are friendly to us. However, most of us readily become a bit complacent at these times.)

LEARN TO LOVE YOURSELF

The most important thing to learn in times of deprivation and lack of fulfilment is to love yourself. Mind you, I didn't say pamper yourself because that only makes you fat and lazy. Loving yourself is more like loving your child. Even if he is not the brightest and even if she is not a beauty you will still love your child intensely. You will give them the best food, the best education you can and lots of cuddles. When they are upset because the other children in the playground teased them you won't scold them. Instead, you will take them in your arms and help them as well as you can.

This is how you have to learn to deal with yourself: don't criticise yourself, don't scold yourself and don't give up on yourself – ever. Instead develop a warm and encouraging feeling towards yourself, no matter how hard your life is, no matter how many setbacks you experience and no matter how many people reject you. The Buddha said, 'You, yourself, as much as anybody in the entire universe, deserve your love and affection.'

If you can love yourself in this way you will easily feel the same kinds of feelings to others because you will realise that everybody wants to be treated in this way. And that is the moment when the positive circle of karma is set into motion, because the love and appreciation you give to others will invariably come back.

If you want to learn even more about unconditional happiness, now is the time to find an experienced teacher and to learn to meditate. Beneath our sadness, beneath our anger and confusion, is such a wealth of indestructible happiness and love, you wouldn't believe it. When you meditate you can discover a glowing sun of love and bliss that is constantly radiating in the depth of your being. If you discover this light you will probably still pursue your wishes, but then you can do it with even more joy and you will be even more successful.

If you don't want to meditate at this moment, don't worry. You don't have to (although it is a real pity if you don't). In order to be successful with wish-practice you don't need to be an accomplished yogi. However, you need to accept that living is learning and you need to find out what you can learn from your current situation in order to let go of your craving. Maybe you need to learn to relax more – join a relaxation class. Maybe you need to develop more self-confidence and to be more assertive with your needs. There is help for all these learning goals – you can be happy, you only need to keep at it.

GIVE YOURSELF A BREAK

The final piece of advice I can give you on how to let go of
your craving is to take regular breaks from wish-practice.
Making your wishes come true doesn't depend solely on
yourself and you don't need to be totally in control of the
whole process. On the contrary, if you have done your bit
you need to get out of the way! Step back, so that the mystery
of things 'popping' into existence can take place.

Even if you are not sure whether you have done enough
to make your wish come true, take regular intervals of 'wish-
practice holidays'. Go down to the pub, meet friends, pursue
a hobby, concentrate on your work or take a real holiday. Do
anything, but don't engage with your desire 'all' the time.
No matter how tempting it is to visualise your wish almost
constantly, no matter how much you want to work all your
time on its fulfilment – don't do it! You will only get in the
way of the magic that will finally fulfil your desire.

It is as if your wish-fulfilling gem can only work secretly
and it can only bring about your wish at a moment when you
look away. So if you are constantly staring at your beautiful
jewel while murmuring your wish-fulfilling spells there will
be no space for it to work magic.

Sometimes people get worried if they forget their wish for
a while because they have become engrossed with something
else. There is nothing to worry about – on the contrary,
forgetting your wish once in a while is highly beneficial. It
gives the primordial ground the right condition to bring
things and situations out into existence.

You really need both: you need to work for your heart-
wish as passionately as you can (yang) *and* you need to step
back and to surrender all control to the secret mechanisms
of bringing things from the primordial ground into existence (yin). So relax and let your wish-fulfilling gem do its
work.

STEP 5, OVERCOMING YOUR CRAVING: THE ESSENTIALS

The biggest obstacle in wish-practice is craving, which is basically every negative feeling around your wish like painful longing, frustration and impatience. Step 5 of wish-practice explains how you can let go of these feelings without suppressing yourself and without letting go of your wish altogether. Instead you will learn how to pursue your wishes with genuine equanimity and joyful anticipation.

- In wish-practice there are two phases. In the yang phase you need to work actively for your wish (Steps 2 to 4 of wish-practice) and in the yin phase you need to step back and let things happen of their own accord without interfering any more. It's like remembering a name – if you try too hard it will never work.

- In order to let go of your craving you need to accept that the universe doesn't owe you a nice life. There is nobody to blame and there is no need to be angry or to pity yourself. Instead you can now fully concentrate on making your wishes come true.

- Accept that every wish has its own time-scale for coming true in the same way as every seed has its own time-scale to grow into a flowering plant. Impatience won't make plants grow faster, nor will it make your wishes come true any more quickly.

- Don't just *try* to let go of your craving, because you can easily end up suppressing yourself. Instead try to find a different focus for your mind that distracts you successfully from obsessing.

- Focus on raising your vibration by concentrating on what you have to offer other people.

- Imagine how your life would develop if your wish did not come true and learn to make your peace with that by using symbol therapy.

- Surrender control to your Higher Consciousness but understand that it can only *assist* you in making your wishes come true. You still have to do the main bit of the work yourself.

- Focus on having fun and develop some self-deprecating humour. Imagine you are the hero or heroine of your favourite sitcom and join in with the audience's laughter about your mishaps in wish-practice.

- Learn to be grateful about *everything* in your life.

- Focus on what you can learn in your pre-wish-fulfilled time.

- Give yourself regular breaks from pursuing your wish.

Step 6

Dealing with the Waiting Time

If you ask me how long it will take to make your wishes come true I can tell you that wish-practice works instantly – in a way. As soon as you utter your wish the whole universe conspires and works on its fulfilment. Unfortunately this 'preparation' can take some time. How long this time will be, nobody knows for sure: it might go very quickly or it might take a little longer. In my experience it is those wishes that are a challenge to our beliefs that will take longest.

One of our deepest beliefs is how much love and happiness is possible for us and others, and it is not easy to trust deeply and believe that we could be *much* happier and *much* more loving (and of course getting *much* more love back). For example, can you believe that you could make *much* more money in a job in which you are *much* happier and in which you can bring *much* more happiness to other people? It's a challenging thought, isn't it?

In my own life the time from making a wish until it came true varied between a few weeks and several years. (I mean here the kinds of wishes for *much* more love and happiness, and not little wishes like 'I wish I could have a pepperoni pizza soon.')

How Long Will it Take?

The fulfilment of wishes depends on so many factors that it is impossible to predict when they will finally manifest. First of all, there are always other people involved in our wishes and, as we hopefully all know, those people can't be controlled. If you want to buy a farm with stables in the countryside, for example, you need to find an estate, and the people who live there need to be ready to move out. This again will depend on a lot of factors in their own lives.

The strings of involvement in making your own personal wish come true are endless and it is really a miracle if finally everything falls into place. How long that will take, nobody can tell, and many wishes involve a shorter or a longer period of waiting.

If you want to get a book published, for example, you can work on it diligently and then you can send it off to publishers. However, after that you have to *wait*. Then you might get a lot of rejections back and you might have to send your typescript to even more publishers. Then you have to *wait* again. Annoying, isn't it? This waiting time can be a big challenge and you can perceive it as a test that will show you whether you have learnt your previous lessons of wish-practice.

If you become frustrated and you start to complain about the unfairness that every idiot can get published, whereas your excellent work is completely ignored, you need to repeat Step 5 and let go of your craving. If you get discouraged and you want to give up on your wish, you need to repeat Step 1 to find your heart-wish. If you interpret all these rejections as the universe wanting to tell you that it is not going to happen for you, you've completely misunderstood the whole idea of wish-practice. In this case you have to read the Introduction again: how wish-practice works.

You need to understand that the universe is not in charge of your life; nobody is. The only person who can and *is able to* make your wishes come true is you. *You* are the one and only guiding force in your life. No matter how many bad omens you seem to perceive, no matter how many unfortunate coincidences seem to block your way, *you* can make your wishes come true by painstakingly working with all eight steps of wish-practice. Quite often this will involve a period of waiting that you have to accept patiently and you need to be able to resist the impulse to plunge into hopelessness or anger.

This waiting time is not just an empty stretch that is nothing but a nuisance. The opposite is true. The time that you are waiting for the fulfilment of your wish can be a time of enormous inner growth. You are opening up to trust a much bigger vision than you have ever thought is possible. You are developing the muscles of your wish-power and you are becoming much more loving and giving through focusing on the altruistic side of your wish. In other words, while working with wish-practice you will become happier, more attractive and more in charge of your life than ever.

All you need to do while you wait is patiently to go through all the previous steps of wish-practice and make sure that you apply them in the right way. Is your heart-wish bold and exciting (Step 1)? Do you practise the wish-practice method regularly and do you keep up your faith by focusing on how you want to contribute to the world with your wish (Step 2)? Do you work for your wish and accept any kind of help that is available to you (Step 3)? Do you focus on love and on what you can do for others with your wish so that you become a happier and more attractive person (Step 4)? And do you patiently let go of your cravings and frustration each time they arise (Step 5)? Well, then you have reason to be happy, because it is only a matter of time before your wish will come true.

But please don't think that you have to be perfect to make your wishes come true. Even if you crave, even if you feel hopeless and despairing, and even if you don't do enough to make your wishes come true, it won't matter so much as long as you can return again and again to a more appropriate attitude. We are all on our way and nobody is a finished product. It is important that you allow yourself to make mistakes and to see yourself as a learner in your field rather than expecting to be perfect and then not trying at all.

I make loads of these mistakes myself but they don't bother me much because I find it more important to experiment and to try things out. Only if my mistakes become too obvious do I tell myself, 'Ulli, if you want to write clever books about how everybody should behave you should at least *try* to adhere to these rules yourself!' If I am lucky this works, and then I become a little bit more patient and serene.

It is helpful to think of a wish as a seed that you have sown that has its own predetermined time to germinate, grow and finally flower. You need to nurture and care for your seedling as well as you can, but there is nothing you can do to make your plant flower much earlier than it is meant to. Some wishes come true within days, while others take a nerve-racking amount of time for no apparent reason and although you obey all the instructions of wish-practice to the letter. Some wishes can even take lifetimes and this isn't a cheat, honestly.

If people had never wished to be able to cure infectious diseases we would still die like flies with every outbreak of bronchitis. Some people even wanted to fly to the moon and their wish came true too, as you know. And other people wanted to be one with God, and the truly enlightened masters of the Earth, such as numerous Tibetan yogis and yoginis, are the proof that their wish has come true as well.

I know from my own experience that we often can't appreciate that there is a perfect timing of each wish when we are in the middle of our wish-practice. 'Why didn't I get this great job?' we moan, and we feel tempted to throw our wish-fulfilling gem against the wall to make it more obedient. However, our jewel will not be impressed by tyrannical behaviour, so it is best to control our temper. In many cases only after we have received our wish can we understand why everything took so long and why we had to endure all these puzzling twists and turns.

Many years ago when I lived in Germany, I was working in a job that was limited to twelve months so I had to look for another one during that year. My chances were good because there were quite a few jobs available in my field. So I applied – and was rejected. I applied again, was accepted – and lost the job at the last minute because there was an internal applicant who was given priority. So it went on for several months and I got more rejections than I had ever had before. I was confused and frustrated. Then a good friend of mine told me about a job vacancy in her office and I was thrilled. 'This is my dream job,' I rejoiced. 'Now I know why I got all these other rejections – I was meant to work with my dear friend!'

I applied and the boss of her company was really enthusiastic about me – and I was rejected shortly afterwards because of internal politics that were beyond the influence of everybody involved. Now I was really frustrated because I couldn't understand why the world had conspired against me. However, I had to go on applying and continued being rejected, and in the end I became unemployed despite a whole year of searching for a job in a pretty good work market. But strangely, despite my job plight my mood was better than ever.

Then came the moment when I finally got to understand the 'reason' behind my mishap. Only two weeks after my job had finished I met my future husband, and within days we both knew that I would move to England to be with him, which I did only six months later. As you can see, everything was perfect timing although I hadn't been able to understand it for the world while I was in the middle of it. There are many more stories like this I could tell you, and you have probably heard or experienced similar things yourself.

In the following sections you can read more about the challenges and pitfalls of the waiting time and how you can master them successfully.

HOW TO DEAL WITH SETBACKS

Out of a thousand people only a hundred embark on the journey to make bold wishes come true. Out of those, ninety-nine experience setbacks, and ninety give up after the first or second problem because they just can't take the frustration any more. So in the end only ten out of a thousand people will successfully achieve major changes in their lives.

I have freely estimated these numbers by looking at all the people I know and I find them quite sad. Why have only nine people out of ninety-nine the perseverance to go through setbacks undeterred? Our wishes are bound to be fulfilled because this is the way the universe works and still so many people give up and continue to live mediocre or even miserable lives because they can't stomach a few frustrations.

In my research about who is most successful in making their wishes come true I have come to the conclusion that there are two sorts of people who have a distinct advantage. The first group comprises those rare people who have an unshakeable sunny and optimistic attitude, which they apply to any of their endeavours. With this kind of positive mood they are very capable of dealing with frustrations and setbacks elegantly. However, there are not many of these indestructible optimists around.

The other group with an advantage is very different. These are people who experienced a lot of suffering and hardship early on in their lives; many of them have a great amount of resilience and are well equipped to deal with setbacks and frustrations later on in life. Therefore they usually make up a significant proportion of the ten people who succeed with wish-practice.

When I began my work as a drugs counsellor I expected that most of my clients would have had awful childhoods just like most people do who buy into the myth that an unhappy childhood leads to an unhappy adulthood. How surprised I was to find that almost the opposite was true! I worked for years with addicts and their parents and found that in many cases it wasn't abuse and neglect that drove children into addiction – it was more or less the opposite, namely over-protection and over-caring. More than once I visited thirty-something addicts in the homes where they lived with their parents, who cooked for them, cleaned up after them and provided them with money for their drugs on a regular basis.

However, it is by no means the case that there are no addicts who had terrible traumas and neglect in their past. I have met plenty of those as well. I was just astonished at how many came from over-protected backgrounds, which made them unable to stomach any kind of hardship and to seek refuge in the easy pleasure of drugs.

Many people who have been pampered and over-protected find it difficult to get to grips with the unavoidable hardships of 'real' life. However, if you were very spoilt as a child there is no need to despair. You just need to understand that the ease and comfort of your childhood is not likely to continue into your adult life unless you learn to persevere despite setbacks and frustrations. You are always better off accepting that life is hard and putting on your sturdy walking-boots to scramble over all of life's obstacles. Then and only then will you be able to deal with the possible setbacks in wish-practice and make your biggest wishes come true.

Many people who start working with wish-practice feel puzzled about the fact that they experience rejections and setbacks at all. 'Shouldn't wish-practice lead me straight to my desired aim?' they wonder. Well, wish-practice *would* lead you to your wish straight away, if you would only allow it to. However, because you get so attached to all the possi-bilities that are *not* the fulfilment of your dream *these possibilities* will reject *you* and then you wonder why. Wish-practice is a wonderful double-edged sword because it works in two ways, as follows.

Wish-practice attracts what you want and *repulses* whatever is not in alignment with your wish at the same time. What seems to be a rejection might actually serve the perfect fulfilment of your dream.

Do you remember all the rejections I got when I looked for a job in Germany? They were actually serving me well, because just around the next corner was waiting my husband-to-be and with him the possibility to work for myself. In actual fact, I had visualised working for myself for many years. As you can see, despite my lack of understanding, my own wish-practice had taken away from me all the opportunities to start working in an employed job, which I would have had to give up only six months later anyway, thereby causing frustration to my employer and my clients.

If you are looking for your soul-mate and you wonder why you get more rejections than ever – now you know the reason. You will reject or *be rejected* by any potential partner who doesn't completely fit your wish-list. This will happen, whether you are aware of the disadvantages of someone or not. Like myself you might think you have found the dream person or the dream job only to find that some quirky co-incidences make this short-term wish impossible. This is not God punishing you – it is your own deep wishes that you carry around with you for quite a while that will deter what is not totally in alignment with your wish-list.

The guiding force in your wish-practice is your own heart-wish and nothing else.

There are quite a few things you should or shouldn't do when you experience setbacks in wish-practice and you can read about these in the following list.

Setbacks and Rejections: Do's

- Tell yourself, 'I am only experiencing this setback or rejection because there is something or someone better for me.' This is not just a cheap consolation but the full truth. Wish-practice *does* work and the reason that you didn't get what you thought was a good opportunity is that this wasn't in total alignment with your wish. For example, a friend of mine was distraught that he couldn't buy a certain flat, only to find three months later that there was a major noise problem there and that he would have been totally unhappy. Through wish-practice you will get in touch with an intuitive guidance you might not notice in any other area of your life.

- View your setbacks as lessons and try to learn from them. Did you try to force something? Were you about to make a bad compromise? Could you have avoided this disappointment if you had scrutinised the situation more?

- If you experience setbacks and disappointments repeat like a mantra, 'I wish that whatever happens is for the highest good of all beings.'

- If you feel very hurt and disappointed focus on raising your vibration. You can do this by wishing for all beings the essence of what you would like to have. If you can do this wholeheartedly you will soon feel better.

- Carry on with your wish-practice method as usual.

Setbacks and Rejections: Don'ts

- Refrain from trying to manipulate the situation with your wish-power by visualising that people make decisions in your favour. I know, it is tempting, but it would be trying to force your will on other people, which can only be detrimental in the long term. Don't try to manipulate a person with your psychic powers to phone you, to feel sexually attracted to you, to give you a job or to sell you an item. Don't do it! Instead repeat like a mantra, 'I wish that whatever happens is for the highest good of all beings' and carry on doing your wish-practice method as usual. If the specific people and situations you are so keen on appear in your visualisation, don't worry. That is OK as long as you know that you just visualise them *as a possibility* or *as a model* but not as a way to secretly manipulate them.

- Don't give up. Setbacks are not a sign from God to tell you that your wish is doomed or that it is 'not meant to be'. On the contrary, setbacks are only a sign that there is something better in store for you and that you have set your heart on something that will ultimately not work. As you go on using wish-practice your intuition will become clearer and you will become more able to find your aim in a more direct way and avoid the setbacks. Therefore go on working with your wish-practice method, raise your vibration and be patient. Consult more people for advice, work with different methods and don't forget to give yourself breaks on a regular basis in order not to become exhausted. When I first tried to get published I received seventy rejections and it would have been very sad if I had given up, thinking 'it is not meant to be', because nearly a year later I suddenly received six letters from interested publishers within one week.

- Don't change and limit your wish out of frustration. If you always wanted to be an artist don't try to tell yourself that it is much more desirable to become an accountant if your artistic aspirations don't work out at first. (But of course you can work as an accountant to finance your artistic career.) You will achieve nothing if you try to talk yourself into wanting something that your parents or your church might think is a good idea but that is *not* what *you* want in your heart of hearts. Instead stick with your heart-wish, even if you have no idea how you could ever realise it. If you regularly work with your wish-practice method and accept all the help that is available to you, you will be surprised how much support you can get. And, don't forget, it is important to maintain a positive and altruistic attitude.

One of my most recent wishes was to buy a new house with my husband and I was very confident when we started our search because I considered myself a 'wish-practice expert'. However, I have been taught a big lesson about getting over-confident because I have never met more setbacks than during our trials to buy this new house. Not only did it take us nearly a year even to find a buyer for our house, but we also just couldn't find a new house that would suit our needs.

After nearly one-and-a-half years of intense searching I finally started to lose my confidence. 'How can I write a book about wish-practice,' I thought miserably, 'if I can't even find a house?' Not only my move was at stake but also my reputation as the 'wish-practice expert'!

Then a beautiful house appeared in the newspaper and a chink of light appeared at the end of the tunnel. We viewed it and instantly 'knew' that this was it – our dream house. We made an offer, told our buyer and were very happy. However, after three days it turned out that our buyer had never been serious about buying our house. So we frantically tried to find a new buyer and even redecorated half our house in a last-ditch attempt to get our dream house.

The weeks went by and nobody turned up who wanted to buy our house, but our dream house didn't find another buyer either. My confidence rose a little bit. Then, finally, we got an offer on our house, but it was far too low to be accepted. There was some toing and froing, and finally our new buyer made an offer that was acceptable. I quickly phoned the estate agent of our dream house to tell him the good news – only to hear that the house had been sold to somebody else the day before. My mood hit rock bottom. (So much for being a wish-practice expert!)

After a while I made some half-hearted attempts to put my own lessons into practice and tried to tell myself that this was only happening because there was a better house for us and that our 'dream house' might have some hidden disadvantages I wasn't aware of. However, despite my trying, I just couldn't believe this. This house had the perfect size, garden and location, and there were definitely no similar houses nearby. I even toyed with the idea of visualising that the deal of the other buyers would fall through (but I didn't do it, honestly!).

When I analysed my situation further I came to the conclusion that all this was teaching me another lesson in humility. Considering myself an expert didn't mean that I was completely in control, and I had to learn to acknowledge the fact that the actual 'magic' of wish-practice is beyond anybody's control (even mine!). So I calmed down, regained my good mood and kept trying to find a new house by focusing on how I could enjoy the house search and on how I could contribute to all beings through our purchase.

Believe it or not, only two weeks later there was this most wonderful house, not even two hundred yards away from the previous one, which was a lot cheaper and which had a much more beautiful garden. We viewed, we made a very generous offer – and we were told that there was so much interest in this house that the estate agent would auction it off! But by now I had learnt my lesson, so I just repeated the mantra 'I wish that whatever happens is for the highest good of all beings ... I wish that whatever happens is for the highest good of all beings'.

When I phoned the estate agent again a few days later, he told me that the auction had been cancelled and that we could probably have the house if we raised our offer to a certain price. This price was still well within our limits, so we got our dream house number two.

The moral: even wish-practice experts are only human beings with lots of flaws.

DEVELOP THE VIRTUE OF PATIENCE

Auntie Mary is back with some more good advice for you!

In many respects wish-practice can be compared with drilling a tunnel through a mountain. In the beginning when your wish is new and exciting you just have soft soil and you will make good progress. But when you have tried for a long time with only small results you have arrived in the middle of the mountain where you'll often find nothing but granite. Many people now make the mistake of turning around and starting a new hole (a new wish) only to find themselves confronted with the same granite a little later.

Don't waste your time scraping shallow dents in the mountainside! Even if you can have instant coffee, Internet banking and all the other devices that help you to get what you want faster and faster, you can't reduce the time of wish-practice any more than you can reduce the time that it takes to be pregnant and to deliver a baby.

Most women who have given birth will probably agree that the time of delivery seems an eternity away when they are at the beginning of the eighth month. But how this differs from wish-practice is that there is no way out at this point. When you are pregnant you have to see it through, no matter how tired or how scared you are. In the same way you have to stick to your wish, and as surely as you will deliver a baby when you are pregnant, you can look forward to the fulfilment of your wish when you work with wish-practice. It just might take some time.

Patience is a virtue that isn't very popular these days and I am not a friend of it either. I really wish I knew a way to make wishes come true more instantaneously as I am very impatient myself. Alas, so far I haven't found the secret. However, I do understand that patience is a virtue because it will protect you from a host of negative feelings created by greed and the inability to wait. So, no matter whether you like or dislike the virtue of patience we are all better off developing some of it.

There is no 'due-date' in wish-practice and the result of our wishing depends a great deal on how much we are able *not* to become impatient and frustrated. Our attitude must be like this: 'If my wish doesn't come true this year then it is fine that it will next year. And if it is not next year I am happy to get what I want the year after. And if it is not then I am happy to wait even longer.'

If you look at your desires in this way there will be no more 'I tried but it didn't work', because there will be only wishes that aren't fulfilled *yet*. However, if you are like most people you might find it difficult to develop this amount of equanimity, and in that case it might be helpful to review Step 5, 'Overcoming your craving'. You can only be successful in wish-practice when you master living with your unfulfilled wish without becoming so frustrated that you want to change it or to give it up.

Sometimes people mistake patience for not really engaging with their wish, for not really wanting it, which is a faulty attitude as well. You need to wish for your desired aim as passionately as it is described in Steps 1 and 2, *and* you need to be patient at the same time. This is like holding a string in your hand and maintaining a certain tension. Imagine the fulfilment of your wish is tied to the other end of the string. If you pull too hard on your string you have fallen into the pitfall of craving, and if you let the string slacken you are too disengaged.

It is perfectly OK to change your wishes when you feel like doing so but it is not wise to change them out of frustration and resignation. The right way to work with wish-practice is to fix your string in your heart and to maintain a gentle tension that gives you a pleasurable tug in your heart which pulls you in the right direction.

TEST HOW FAR YOU HAVE COME

I am sure nobody wants to know how far away their desired aim still is. Oh sorry, you *do* want to know?

OK, for all of you who are dying to find out whether the fulfilment of your wish is anywhere near, there are two tests available that can give you a clue.

The first test will give you immediate feedback and the second test is part of symbol therapy and will give you feedback in the form of inner images *over time*.

Exercise
Test How Near You Are to Your Desired Aim

*Do this as often as you like

- Write on a blank piece of paper, 'My wish for ... [fill in your desired aim] is fulfilled'.

- Say this sentence out loud and try to imagine that it is true. Watch out for an inner response in the form of words ('yes', 'I can't believe it', etc.), feelings (happy, sad or other feelings), inner images or body sensations.

- Write your response underneath your initial sentence.

- Repeat your initial sentence five to ten times and try to imagine that it is true. Each time observe your inner response and write it down.

- Evaluate your results: if your responses were very positive you are not far away from your desired aim. But if your responses were doubtful, fearful or otherwise negative you still have some work to do. Don't worry, these obstacles can be overcome more quickly than you think. The best thing to do is to practise symbol therapy and to raise your vibrations, as explained in Steps 2, 4 and 5.

- Don't repeat your initial sentence like an affirmation in order to break though your inner barriers. By now you should know that this would only activate and strengthen your inner resistance and that you need to be cleverer than that.

The kind of feedback you will receive through this test is not at all scientific, as it will depend a great deal on your current mood. Although most scientists would totally disagree, this subjectivity doesn't lessen the truthfulness of the test at all. On the contrary, as the fulfilment of your (outer) wishes depends a great deal on the state of your (inner) mind, this test will mirror exactly your chances of letting things pop into existence from the primordial ground.

If you are in a bad mood your chances *are* limited and if you are happy your chances *are* indeed better. So, don't worry too much if you didn't get the best results with this test today but try to focus on raising your vibrations. When you feel better you can try again and you will see that your chances will have improved dramatically.

Now to the next test. This is derived from symbol therapy and will give you surprisingly accurate feedback. However, this feedback will become clearer to you only over time.

Exercise
Test How Far You Have Come to the Fulfilment of Your Wish with Symbol Therapy

*Do this whenever you feel like it

- Relax in the way that is convenient to you. (You can use the relaxation at the beginning of the 'World of happiness' exercise on page 48.)

- You are now ready to contact your Higher Consciousness, who will help you to find answers to all of your questions. See your Higher Consciousness as an angelic being or as a beautiful shimmering light that has a living and loving quality. Feel how you are embraced by the love and support of your Higher Consciousness.

- Tell your Higher Consciousness about your wish and how you want to contribute to the world through its fulfilment. See your Higher Consciousness smiling and nodding in agreement with your good motivation.

- Ask your Higher Consciousness to show you a path, a track or a road that leads to the fulfilment of your wish. You might be shown a footpath, a forest track or even a motorway. Please note that at this point your desired aim should not appear in the picture. Ask in the following way, 'Higher Consciousness, can you please show me the path that leads to the fulfilment of my wish?' and just acknowledge the very first thought or idea of a path that comes into your mind.

- When you have received an inner picture thank your Higher Consciousness for its help.

- Repeat this exercise every one or two weeks and observe how you move forward on your path. When your path is flat and beautiful you will have an easy development. But

if your track is rocky and steep you might have to overcome some obstacles. Sooner or later your desired aim
will appear in your inner image and you can be assured
that your wish will be fulfilled soon.

Many people who try the above exercise assume that it is
'just' wishful thinking if they envision a positive development. However, if you try to sincerely tune into your Higher
Consciousness you will be surprised by the accuracy of the
feedback you receive. On a deep level we all have clairvoyant
abilities, which in most people are still dormant. However,
symbol therapy gives you an opportunity to awaken some of
your psychic powers through the use of symbols and inner
images.

A client of mine wished for (guess what!) – a husband.
When she asked for a track to the fulfilment of her desired
aim she was shown a path that led along the coast. For a long
time she saw herself walking alongside the ocean, in the
beginning alone but later on with more and more friends. At
some stage she had the strong intuition that the man of her
dreams was waiting for her just around the next bay and so
she started to speed up her steps in anticipation. My client
was puzzled by her positive images because there was no
attractive man in her life whatsoever. But sure enough, a few
weeks later she did meet a wonderful man whom she
married shortly afterwards.

If you want to make use of the feedback that you can
receive through symbol therapy, you need to approach this
method with a relaxed and playful mind. Don't take the
results deadly seriously but see whether they make sense to
you. If this exercise has given you accurate feedback once or
twice in your life you will be able to trust it more and more
in the future.

A Particular Pitfall in Wish-practice

Quite a few people experience a particular pitfall in wish-practice that only occurs if they have been successful with every other step so far.

When you are sure about your heart-wish and you practise your wish-practice method regularly, and when you work diligently for your aim while being able to let go of all your craving, you might suddenly start to feel very happy in yourself although your wish is as unfulfilled as ever. For people who assume that their entire well-being is tied to the fulfilment of their wish this might come as a big surprise.

Peggy, for example, had wished with all her might to have plenty of clients for her homeopathic practice and her entire self-esteem was bound up with this aim. When she had many clients she felt up, and when she had only a few clients she felt very low. But then something happened that was quite strange for her. While she had worked with wish-practice she started to feel better and better in herself, and her self-confidence rose, even though she still did not have as many clients as she wanted. But suddenly Peggy was able to relax and to read her favourite books without agonising about her homeopathic practice any more and she started to enjoy life to a degree that was unknown to her before. And then Peggy fell into the particular pitfall of wish-practice.

Because Peggy suddenly felt so much better, even though her wish wasn't fulfilled yet, she started to question whether her wish was still important to her and wondered *whether she should give it up*. Peggy's thoughts went something like this: 'If I feel so good in myself anyway, I might as well go back to the security of my job as a secretary and I will not have to worry any more about how to make ends meet with my ailing homeopathic practice.'

Like Peggy, many people who are successfully working with wish-practice consider giving up their aim once they start to feel much better even though their wish isn't fulfilled yet. No matter how much they have desired their goal before, no matter how much work they have already invested, when people feel better they are often tempted to avoid the risks that go along with pursuing their wish, and they opt for the security of their old and familiar life.

But Peggy and everybody else who wants to give up their wish do not realise that it is their very commitment to their wish that is making them so happy. By working for their wish they love themselves and in that way they have a more loving relationship with the world. And this is what has made them so much happier. If they now want to give up their wish, in many cases their well-being will soon collapse like a house of cards.

What I want to say is this: don't give up your wish, no matter whether you feel hopeless and resigned and no matter whether you feel so happy that you think you can do without your wish. Instead, congratulate yourself on coming so far – you can only feel this sense of well-being because you are able to work for your wish while successfully letting go of your craving. Use your happiness to focus even more on the altruistic part of your wish and enjoy the fact that you are now in the state of mind that will make it even more likely that things pop into existence from the primordial ground.

STEP 6, DEALING WITH THE WAITING TIME: THE ESSENTIALS

Step 6 tells you how to deal with the waiting time that is (unfortunately) often part of the journey when you try to make big wishes come true.

- It is impossible to tell in advance when a wish will be fulfilled because there is always a multitude of factors and people involved in any wish.

- The waiting time is not only a nuisance, but also a chance for enormous inner growth if you can make use of this opportunity.

- Go patiently through all the previous steps of wish-practice and make sure that you return to the appropriate attitude every time you lose your way. But don't worry, you don't have to be perfect – just do the best you can.

- If you feel hurt and frustrated by rejections and setbacks remember that wish-practice works in two ways: it *attracts* what you want and it *repels* what is not in alignment with your wish. Rejections are not a sign of your Higher Consciousness showing you that your wish is doomed, but a message that your intuition could do with some more fine-tuning because you still get hooked on the 'wrong' possibilities.

- If you experience setbacks, frustrations and rejections, go through the do's and don'ts lists in order to quickly regain a positive state of mind. Don't abuse your wish-power by trying to manipulate other people for your own advantage.

- Wish-practice is like drilling a tunnel through a mountain. Don't give up every time the going gets tough and start a new hole. Instead develop patience, stamina and resilience.

- Use the two tests (see pages 185 and 187) in order to find out how far you have come in the fulfilment of your wish.

- Don't give up your wish if you have been working so successfully with wish-practice that you have become very happy in yourself.

Step 7

Removing any Remaining Obstacles

The teachings of the Buddha are divided into several major groups and the first two are called small vehicle and great vehicle. Freely interpreted, the small vehicle is about attaining peace of mind. In this group of teachings you learn how to get rid of the things in your life and in your mind that cause you and others to suffer, and you learn to live in a more peaceful and harmonious way by continuously letting go of everything that creates disturbing emotions and suffering. In other words, in the small vehicle you learn to stop being a nuisance to yourself and others. If you are able to do this you will find that life can actually be enjoyed and your world will start to look more like a beautiful garden than a place of war and depression.

When you have achieved more peace and beauty it seems natural to develop the wish and to pass this happiness on to others. This positive wish for others is called love, and when it becomes more important for you, you have entered the great vehicle, which puts its greatest emphasis on altruistic love.

Wish-practice as it is taught in this book is part of the great vehicle because it stresses the importance of contributing in an altruistic way to the world with your wish. And, as I have just explained, in order to be successful with the great vehicle you need to have practised the small one – you need to be able to have at least a minimum peace of mind. If you are imprisoned in addictions or in destructive relationships, if your life is poisoned by guilt, resentment and self-pity, you will find it hard to accomplish the previous six steps of wish-practice.

If you have big problems such as these you will probably not be able to solve them just by reading through the rest of this chapter, and sometimes you will need to find a self-help group or a therapist to get you out of the bog. You can, of course, also work with symbol therapy (as described in Step 2), which is the most effective self-help method that I know. It is described in my book *Symbol-therapy* and can be used by anybody who feels inspired by it.

Generally speaking, you need to throw everything out of your life that creates emotional drama on a regular basis. It is important to have some peace and quiet in your life in order to let things arise from the primordial ground. However, the relaxation that is created through drinking alcohol or taking drugs doesn't really count because that is just numbing yourself. You need to find some *genuine* peace of mind.

With wish-practice you can completely reinvent yourself (I like to think of myself as a totally different person from the one I have been), but wish-practice can't help you to escape from your past. Whatever your background and whatever your past experiences – if you can't make your peace with them they will act as major obstacles to any wish you want to achieve for your future.

Below you will read about the possible obstacles in wish-practice and what you can do about them.

PASSIVELY PUTTING UP WITH NEGATIVITY

Of all the possible obstacles in wish-practice I have seen in the lives of others, and in my own, the obstacle of 'not wishing' is *by far* the most detrimental. As we have already discussed, you can't be without wishes. So if people are in a terrible job or in an unsatisfactory marriage and they don't actively wish for improvement, they are wishing on a deeper and unconscious level that things stay as they are. Isn't that sad?

The worst obstacle in wish-practice is not to wish at all.

Almost any part of your life can be improved for you and the people around you if you follow Steps 1 to 6 of wish-practice. But many people have neither the knowledge nor the courage to do that. They fear that their marriage will break up if they only touch the topic, and they are afraid that they could fail to achieve their aims and be frustrated or even ridiculed by other people.

One of the most common reasons that keeps people from wishing for a better life is the fear of being disappointed in case they fail. 'If I wish for better health or a senior position in a company and I don't get it,' somebody might say, 'I will feel even worse than if I hadn't started to wish at all. But once my desire is awakened it will bother me much more if I don't get what I want.'

There is some truth in this argument. Once you set your heart on something it will be much harder to stay serene and detached than if you had never started consciously wishing for it. But the solution is not to put up with a mediocre or even bad life. The solution is to wish only for those things that are really worth while and will definitely bring you the happiness that you desire. Then you will have the stamina to keep going if your wish is not fulfilled easily.

Only if you focus on real heart-wishes will your life change its course and head towards happiness rather than towards more and more suffering. And once you have chosen your wish you can put your heart at rest because you can rely on the second truth of wish-practice, 'You *will* get what you want'. If you stay with your wish in a committed way without getting angry and frustrated it *will* manifest at some point because this is the way the universe works.

One of the *worst* reasons for not wishing for a better life is the belief that it is easier to put up with bad compromises than to go through the upheaval of changing everything. Behind this attitude is the belief that we just have 'to bear' a few more years until we die and finally find eternal peace. In this way death is seen as the ultimate comforter, like a sweet, deep sleep that liberates us from our worries of the day. Alas, nothing could be further from the truth.

There is no death that rescues us from our earthly problems. On the contrary, once we leave our physical bodies behind we live with even more intensity. In Buddhism it is taught that when we are dead, all our thoughts and emotions become reality. For example, without a physical body, 'thinking' of New York means 'being' in New York, and equally 'thinking' of paradise means 'being' there. Therefore our Buddhist teachers keep admonishing us to develop a loving and wise mind while we are still living at this level of existence. The only reliable rescue we can find from suffering, they tell us, is having altruistic wishes and developing peace of mind.

Let me repeat: not wishing for a better and happier life will not pay off.

Some people don't want to wish for more because they think it is greedy. Again, these people don't realise that they can't be without wishes and that the only way to wish in a beneficial way is to do it consciously. If you have achieved most of what is important for yourself the natural next step is to wish for others. That is what my beloved Buddhist teachers tell and show us. According to them, enlightenment doesn't mean that you can sit there up on your pedestal and just enjoy yourself for ever. Instead it means to love, to heal and to liberate for ever in a spontaneous and effortless way.

Not knowing what to wish for is another common problem. People who experience this are often quite nice, stable fellows. They feel they have life well under control and they don't experience lots of ups and downs. However, in all their stability they have lost a certain edge because everything feels so secure for them that they have lost their sense of adventure.

If you feel like this I recommend that you do something that makes you feel excited or even a bit scared in order to shake yourself out of your complacency. If you don't know what you want you need to be physically active and put yourself into demanding situations. When the pressure rises you might be able to see with more clarity what is really important for you in life. For example, imagine you are going to lose everything and ask yourself what you would want to have back most desperately.

You can also try to write an imaginary obituary for yourself. Do you really want to be known to the people who come after you as 'The person who was known for nothing and who didn't make the slightest difference for themselves or for others'?

UNSUPPORTIVE RELATIONSHIPS

One of my biggest personal obstacles to making my own wishes come true was relating to and even clinging to people who weren't terribly supportive of me and who certainly didn't wish that I could achieve the happiness and success I have now. Funny, isn't it? Why should anybody maintain relationships that are not really loving and supportive? Good question. Now that I have all that behind me I wonder about it myself, and I wonder even more why so many people keep doing just that: being in close relationships with people who are not really supportive of them.

The answer is as simple as it is sad. Most of us would rather stay in relationships that give us illusory feelings of security than risk being all alone if we insist on being treated with ongoing love and respect. The word 'ongoing' is the key. Many people I have spoken to can't even imagine that there could be someone in the universe who could love them *continuously* without ever falling out of this caring and supportive feeling. 'What about arguments?' they ask. 'You can't possibly expect that you will never have any conflicts!' No, I don't expect to never have conflicts, but I talk about arguing with your partner without hostile feelings and while continuing to love each other. This is perfectly possible and if you don't have relationships like this it will be hard to achieve bigger breakthroughs in wish-practice.

The quality of your relationships is the direct outcome of your most important and possibly unconscious beliefs and wishes. And your relationships are the fertile field, so to speak, in which all your other wishes can grow. Let me put it a bit more drastically – you just can't expect to be very happy in your job, in doing your art or as a parent if you have a partner who hates you.

You can spend thousands of hours meditating on love and peace, but you will not harvest many positive results from your practice if you have a partner who involves you in an argument as soon as you leave your meditation cushion. The emotional atmosphere of your primary relationships will mainly dictate how you will feel in any other area of your life, no matter how much you work with wish-practice, no matter how much therapy you have and no matter how much you meditate.

But please don't blame your partner if you are not successful with wish-practice, because your relationship with them was *and still is* your own wish. If you want to change a negative relationship there is only one way: you need to wish for a more loving relationship, stick to your wish and do all you can to make it happen, while keeping in mind that you can't change your partner against their will. In other words, you need to take the risk that your unsupportive relationship breaks up and to go a part of your journey alone until you have found someone who you can love and who really loves you.

This is exactly what I have done and I can reassure you that it was absolutely worth it.

However, the situation is a bit more complicated if you have difficult relationships with people you can't just leave behind, such as members of your family, or colleagues at work, for instance. The best thing to do is to reduce difficult relationships like these as far as you can to the areas that work and to avoid topics of disagreements as much as possible. You also have to learn to give yourself the support that you would normally expect from a boss or a parent, for example, and to let go of your negative feelings. If this is very difficult it can be useful to find someone who supports you in this process.

JEALOUSY

In Buddhism feelings like jealousy are called poisons of the mind and indeed they are. Jealousy feels awful and it is also an obstacle for your wish-practice. Even the most perfect life can be poisoned through this negative emotion because there is always someone who has more or something better. But jealousy is such a superfluous attitude and it can easily be overcome.

If you suffer from jealousy first of all forgive yourself. It is not a crime and not a reason to stop loving yourself. So whisper into your inner ear that you will always love yourself even if you will keep envying other people. If you are a very self-critical person (which is likely if you are jealous) developing some love for yourself should take away the first layer of suffering.

Next, try to realise that anybody whom you envy could be as jealous as you with other people (or even with you!) because there is no perfect situation for any human being. Even if someone is beautiful their body could always be improved upon. Even if someone is rich, there is always space for more need for money. And even if someone has the best of careers and fame there are always others who are doing better. So if the person you envy doesn't envy others it isn't for the reason that they just 'have' everything, because this is impossible in the human world. It is for the simple reason that they know how to deal with jealousy and how to overcome it effectively.

The best way to overcome jealousy is to see the person who brings this green colour into your face as a model or as a teacher. If you can appreciate and admire the qualities of this person you can open yourself up to their energy field, and in this way you will be able to participate in their good qualities and to develop them in yourself without effort.

For example, if you envy a man who has a stunning career and who is always surrounded by the prettiest women, it will poison your mind. This means that you will be even less attractive to women and your career will not profit from your inner negativity either. But if you can genuinely admire this man, some of his attractiveness and charm will pass over to you, women will like you more and your career will improve as well. Anyone you envy, for whatever reason – if you can genuinely admire their qualities you are developing them in yourself at that very moment!

I expect some of you will find it hard to believe what I've just described. There is only one cure for this: try it out. Instead of hating the victim of your envy, start to appreciate and admire them. The more you can do this with a genuinely open heart, the more positive qualities you will receive from this person. In this way jealousy will be transformed from a poison in your mind into a genuine friend.

RESENTMENT AND GRUDGES

Resentment and smouldering grudges are more feelings
that can be big obstacles to your wishes coming true. Why is
that? Why can't you be angry with some people (who really
deserve it, of course) without losing your ability to make
your own wishes come true?

The primordial ground from which everything arises is
your own heart-mind and if this space is filled even partially
with anger and resentment (no matter how much these feelings seem to be justified), your primordial ground is
poisoned by these emotions and it can't bring something
about that will make you deeply happy.

Many people who wish for a partner, for example, don't
realise how much they hinder themselves by their lingering
resentment of their previous partner. The same is true if you
harbour grudges for your former boss and even for a neighbour.

The most detrimental effect of grudges you can create is
when you resent your own parents. Our bonds with our
parents are so intricate and complex that we will never be
able to escape them. If we hate our parents, even with feelings of harmless-looking resentment, we are hating
ourselves and in that way we will never be able to achieve
real happiness. It is a real shame that in some therapies
people are encouraged to feel these negative feelings
towards their parents, because this will create even more
suffering. The real solution is learning to forgive and to let
go of old grudges.

Unfortunately there is much confusion about forgiveness.
It does *not* mean condoning the behaviour of the person who
behaved badly. It does *not* mean dissolving or taking away
the guilt from this person. Of course you would report it to
the police if someone did something unlawful to you or the
people around you.

Forgiveness simply means that you stop bearing the

grudge and the resentment because it is poisoning *yourself*. Only if you receive a sincere apology from the person who has harmed you can you be close to them again. In all other cases you will need to let go the person who has harmed you with your blessing.

The following exercise will show you how you can get rid of any resentment that is still poisoning your life and hampering your wish-practice.

Exercise
Let Go of Old Grudges

***Do this as often as you need it**

- Make a list of all your family members, your former partners and all other people who were important to you in your life, no matter whether they are still alive or not.

- See in your mind all these people one by one entering your room and notice how you feel about them. When you feel repulsion, fear and anger you will need to let go your resentment.

- Say to every person you feel negative towards, in turn, '[name], although I still don't condone what you did and although I still wish you would change your behaviour I stop resenting you and I give you your freedom.' See in your mind a sharp and gleaming sword cutting through the ties of anger and begrudging that are still binding you to this person. (The real tie in a relationship is hatred – only love will give both of you the freedom to each go your own way.)

- If you were in a close relationship with someone you felt resentment towards (like a former partner, for example) write or speak to them personally and tell them that you

don't harbour any bad feelings towards them any more
and that you wish them all the best.

• If the people who have harmed you apologise, you are
  lucky because then it is probably much easier to let go of
  your grudge.

• If the people who have harmed you deny their guilt it is
  much more difficult to set them free because a part of
  you will continue to cling to them in search of compen-
  sation. (That is very human, don't worry.) In this case
  you can pray to your Higher Consciousness to send an
  angel to this person. Ask for an angel who will love this
  person, who will help them and most of all who will
  better them. Think of this angel every time your mind
  wants to return to your old detrimental feelings of
  resentment. Over time your negative feelings will
  dissolve and you will be free finally to make your most
  desired wishes come true.

'But what if someone has done something awful to you, like
abused you or even killed your child,' somebody might ask,
'you can't possibly forgive them?'.

I believe that our ability for compassion and forgiveness is
much bigger than we usually experience. I have heard
several reports of Tibetan people who endured torture by
their Chinese occupiers, while continuously maintaining a
compassionate attitude towards them.

These Tibetan people believed deeply in the law of karma
that dictates that everybody will get back what they give out,
and they even felt sorry for their torturers because they
knew that they were creating the most terrible future for
themselves.

GUILT

If you have done something in the past that was wrong, like stealing or being violent or hateful, it will stand in the way of making your wishes come true. This is not because God wants to punish you for it but because your own bad conscience (even if you are completely unaware of it) will not allow you to achieve greater happiness in life.

When I was a drugs counsellor I worked both with battered wives and with their violent partners. For a while I didn't know who I should pity most, but later on I realised that the guilty party is in by far the worse position. It is a myth to believe that you can do awful things to others and then live a happy life. If this seems to be the case one can only see a very superficial layer of the truth.

As a counsellor I had the opportunity to talk to people who had done really bad things to others and found they were extremely unhappy. One example was a university professor who had killed somebody in a car accident and who knew that it had been his own fault. However, he had been able to hire a famous solicitor, who had bailed him out and he hadn't received any punishment at all.

I observed that this man, and others who had severely harmed others, kept punishing *themselves* by ruining their careers, their marriages and their health. On the other side, the victims of violent action I encountered were much more positive because they had at least the advantage of being in a morally better position.

If you have left a former partner in a hateful way, if you have hit your child too hard in a rage or if you have stolen money from your company, you don't need to despair – you will still be able to be successful with wish-practice. But you do need to repair the damage that you have done in order to find the happiness you desire. Otherwise the power of your own bad conscience will be stronger than you might think and your deep-seated guilt feelings will not

allow you to really find what you wish for, no matter how
hard you try.

In order to repair your guilt you need to apologise
sincerely; you need to pay back what you have taken and you
need to make good anything you have done as well as you
can. It is best if you can do this openly and directly.
However, if contacting former partners or other people you
have harmed would cause even more hurt, you need to be
creative and find a way to make things good more subtly.

You can pray for people, you can give money to charity on
their behalf and you can talk to them lovingly just in your
mind. The next move is to promise never to do it again. If
you can do all this you can be assured that your guilt will be
erased and that you will now be free to find the life of your
dreams.

Some people carry guilt feelings around that are unnecessary, but that cause them a lot of suffering. For example, I
know a woman who feels guilty about the mere fact that she
has money and a comfortable life. These kinds of feelings
can also be a hindrance to making your dreams come true
and you can read in the next section what you can do about
them.

INABILITY TO RECEIVE

An inability to receive anything good can be a severe
problem and it mainly afflicts 'goody-goody' people. (Do you
remember, goody-goody people are those who work on
themselves and who want to lead a spiritual life?) Alongside
their spiritual and compassionate ideals many of these
people carry strong ideas of their own unworthiness, which
is very sad because they are actually very worthy – if not the
worthiest of all.

I have met social workers who were deeply unhappy in
their jobs but who wouldn't allow themselves to see clients

privately, because they were unable to accept even a moderate amount of money for their work. I have seen numerous spiritual seekers who didn't allow themselves to have a sexual relationship, let alone a family, because they were afraid of failing on their spiritual path if they experienced 'worldly' joys. I have seen wonderful people ruining their lives through addiction and through antagonising anybody who was trying to help them because of their deep-seated self-hatred.

If you feel like that you need first of all to develop some love for yourself. Don't worry that loving yourself could make you egotistical or even arrogant – the opposite is true. Loving yourself will make you able to love others even more. And, what is best, your love and care for others will not be a tiring chore any more because it will flow much more naturally and effortlessly.

Here is an exercise for developing more love for yourself, which I use almost routinely on most of my clients, and which has never failed to bring positive results. Even the most self-loathing person softened when trying it. However, the exercise will only work for you if you do it on a regular basis.

Exercise
Developing More Love for Yourself

Do this as often as you need it

- Remember a moment in your life when you deeply loved someone. You might have felt this love for your baby, a partner or a pet.

- When you feel this love, just turn it towards yourself without thinking about it a lot and without changing it. Feel love for yourself and enjoy it at the same time.

- Start to talk to yourself in the same loving way that you would talk to someone you love. Speak about your problems and wishes in a compassionate, soothing way like you would talk to a small, beloved child.

- Tell yourself that there is nothing wrong with accepting the goodness of life and that you deserve it as much as anybody else. Encourage yourself to get over any feelings of unworthiness.

- Do this exercise frequently and in many situations until it becomes second nature.

REGRET

The little brother of guilt is regret, which includes ongoing grief for a breakdown of a relationship, for a split-up with a business partner or a bankruptcy in your business. These feelings of regret are a mixture of grief, guilt and melancholic longing that things should have gone otherwise, and they can be a big hindrance to making a new beginning and fulfilling your wishes.

If you suffer from this condition you need to practise loving and forgiving yourself on a regular basis. Do the above exercise for developing love for yourself so often that it becomes second nature. Try to realise that you don't benefit anybody if you keep yourself from becoming happy again, least of all your children, if they are involved. Children always learn best from models, and if you can show them how to get through a major trauma in life and get out the other side with a happy face you will help them tremendously to cope with the traumas that they might have to face one day.

Talk to supportive people about your regrets as much and as often as you need to get the reassurance that you have the right to move on to start a new and happier life. Don't punish yourself if you had a major break-up by henceforth living a minimal life. Remember the words of the Buddha: 'You, yourself, as much as anybody in the entire universe, deserve your love and affection.'

SELF-PITY

The complementary attitude to guilt and regret is self-pity, and it is at least as detrimental as the other obstacles. This 'I am such a poor thing syndrome' will make it hard for you to get out of bed and tackle your dreams because you feel so unfairly treated and disadvantaged.

There can be something deeply comforting and safe in pitying yourself. At least you know that you are down and that the rest of the world is trampling over you. Self-pity is painful, but on the positive side it gives stability. However, if you want to change your life you need to give up the comfort of feeling stable and self-righteous in your misery. You need to move around like the rest of us, take risks and face frustrations, and you need to defend yourself against other people who try to take advantage of you.

The best way to transform self-pity is to turn it into self-care. This requires only a little twist in your attitude, because self-pity is really a distorted form of self-love. Imagine that your daughter is in trouble. Surely you wouldn't just pity her. You would comfort her lovingly, but then you would get up and do something to help her. In the same way you need to love and comfort yourself, but then you have to get up in order to change your detrimental circumstances – wish-practice is an excellent tool for doing just that.

Next you need to give up the belief that you need to suffer because something awful has happened to you in the past. No matter how justified this attitude appears – it is *not* true!

Most people experience dreadful things at least once in their lives. The difference between happy and unhappy people is that happy ones can transform their self-pity into self-care while unhappy ones get stuck in their negative feelings. If you look at the biographies of very successful people it is amazing how many of them came from very hard or disadvantaged backgrounds, and how many of them had suffered great losses in their lives.

Come on, throw this debilitating self-pity away and join the crowd of unfairly treated and disadvantaged people who are still able to create wonderful lives for themselves and the people around them.

Too Much Chaos, Clutter and Distraction

How can anybody have major wishes manifest in their life while they are up to their neck in chaos, stress and clutter, and the few remaining minutes of their free time are totally filled with 'important' activities like watching soap operas, drinking too much alcohol and going shopping for the fifth time in a week?

How can anybody find a new partner while they are deeply immersed in the emotional drama of an existing relationship?

How can anybody find time for their own wishes while doing a thousand things for others, which they could perfectly well do for themselves?

I really don't know!

Generally speaking, people only do things if they assume that at the bottom line they are getting something out of it. So, if you find yourself surrounded by so much chaos, demand and clutter that you can't find any space and time to work for your wish, you need to ask yourself what you get out of this situation. Don't say 'nothing'. Everybody gets something out of their behaviour, no matter how mad, how self-destructive and how stupid it might look from the outside. For example, having lots of stress might protect you from being bored, from feeling useless and from the big black hole into which you could suddenly disappear if you didn't keep yourself constantly occupied.

Having lots of dependent people around you who eat up the last of your energy reserves protects you from looking into the mirror and answering the difficult question, 'Who am I and what do *I* want in this world?' Eating a whole packet of biscuits in front of your favourite soap opera can successfully help you to take your mind off the fear that arises when you think of the next step you need to take in order to make your wish come true.

Can you see, all this behaviour is perfectly logical if you look at it a little bit more closely. So, if you have all this clutter in your life, can you now say how it serves you?

Even if you still don't know the answer to this question, you need to understand that in order for your wish to manifest you need to have some space. If you are totally preoccupied with a thousand things, how can your wish find a place in your life?

You could start by tidying up your home. Then go on and tidy up the things you have to do each day with the help of a proper daily work planner. Learn to do only those things for others on a regular basis that they really can't do for themselves because otherwise you will just make these people dependent on you. In a last step you need to tidy up your relationships. Only relate closely to those people who are totally supportive of you and your aims. Keep a little bit more distance from everyone else.

I promise you that you will find more space in your life when you do all this tidying up, and I promise you as well that this space will at first feel a little bit scary. After all, the reason why most people create all this stress is to avoid the fear of feeling alone and without purpose in the universe.

However, once you have got a little bit used to more time and quiet for yourself, you will discover that it is actually a blessing. It is only from here that your creative ideas can arise. And it is only from here that you can learn to redefine yourself and to create a life that suits your needs and the needs of the people around you in a much better way than the hectic life you lived before.

STEP 7, REMOVING ANY REMAINING OBSTACLES: THE ESSENTIALS

Step 7 deals with all the remaining problems that could be in the way of making your dreams come true. Basically, you need to throw anything out of your life that creates emotional drama on a regular basis, in order to achieve at least a minimum of peace of mind.

- The worst obstacle to creating a better life is not to wish at all, because that means that on a more unconscious level you wish that everything stays as it is.

- The quality of your primary relationships determines the overall emotional quality of your life, so it is crucial to create positive relationships with supportive and loving people.

- Jealousy, a common but damaging attitude, can be overcome by seeing the person you envy as a model or a teacher. In that way the envied qualities of this person will pass over to you without effort.

- Grudges and resentment can block all other efforts in wish-practice, so it is crucial to completely let them go and to make peace with anybody who might have harmed you in the past.

- If you have done something wrong in the past, you need

to repair it because your own bad conscience will otherwise not allow you to achieve greater happiness.

- Some people feel so unworthy that they are not able to
receive anything good. They need more than anything to
develop a loving attitude towards themselves.

- Lingering regrets about things that went wrong in your
life can stop you from making a new beginning. You need
to learn to love and forgive yourself in order to let them
go.

- Self-pity can be overcome by turning it into self-care.

- Too much stress and chaos will clutter up your life so that
your wish will not find any space to manifest. You need to
tidy up your life in every respect to create some peace and
quiet.

Step 8

Receiving the Fulfilment of Your Wish

Ah – now we come finally, finally to the best step of wish-practice – receiving the fulfilment of your wish! I would like to be able to tell you that from now on life will be all a bed of roses: you receive your wish like a gigantic birthday present and then you live happily ever after. Alas, it isn't quite that easy for many people (although it may well be for some).

Before you can finally settle down with your magic parcel you need to be able to distinguish it from all the other parcels, which look equally enticing, but which are nothing but fakes.

DON'T MAKE BAD COMPROMISES

When you are working with wish-practice you will discover that the universe offers you many possible 'wish-fulfilments', and that it is *your* task to choose from these possibilities and to reject whatever is not completely in alignment with your heart-wish. You will also discover that as you come nearer and nearer to your aim, 'the offers' get better and better, so that it will be even more difficult to decide what option you will finally settle down with. You may have to decide many times whether you have finally found your heart-wish, or whether you should hang on for a little while and wait for something or someone even better.

These decisions can sometimes be really agonising. As a friend of mine puts it, 'You are presented with a succession of ever-more delicious puddings and you can't really tuck into any of them'. She is right: you can't always eat all these puddings. You must make a decision whether to take on the job in the US or to stay here and wait for a better one. You can't do both. Nor can you start a serious relationship with several people at the same time or buy many things simultaneously. In other words, when you finally come near the fulfilment of your wish there is a vast potential for making the wrong choice and settling for second best because you don't have enough courage, faith and patience to wait for something or someone that *really* suits your needs.

If you are like most people you will have a tendency to settle for second best because it is 'unrealistic, greedy and selfish' to wait for something really, really wonderful. I am sure auntie Mary would totally agree with this opinion and would advise you to go with the safe and sensible option, instead of waiting for your 'unrealistic' dream to come true.

It's not that I dislike auntie Mary, but sometimes I totally disagree with her. Why work through a whole book of wish-practice if in the end you are prepared to settle for the sensible and 'realistic' solution? You can do better than that! My advice is: go for the full monty and have nothing for a while rather than settle for a second-best solution.

Empty stretches almost always feel scary and unsatisfactory, but in hindsight they are often the most productive times of our lives. In these phases we are training and developing the muscles of our heart-mind as at no other time by working with all the steps of wish-practice. You can develop a wonderful vision and the trust that this vision will come true. You can experience more unconditional love and happiness than you had ever thought possible. And you can discover in the depth of your being a wealth of goodness and intuitive wisdom that would have stayed hidden if everything had been continuously served to you on a silver tray.

I myself don't like these empty stretches, but I do value the increased strength, wisdom and unconditional happiness that usually arise from them if I can see these times as challenges rather than as a nuisance. In case you have forgotten how to master the challenge of having to wait, please go back to Step 6, 'Deal with the waiting time'.

There is a great strength in the ability to say 'No' to bad compromises and to stay true to your wish. If you say 'No' to every ball life throws at you this would just be a continuation of your old negative pattern, and if you can stay committed to the one outcome of your wish that would truly make you happy, you can expect amazing transformations in your life. You will surprise all your friends and family by your ongoing 'good luck' that seems to defy all their beliefs of what is possible, and you will be baffled yourself by how much you and your life can change. Let me put it this way, if you can stay uncompromising and totally committed to your wish you can become the hero or heroine of your self-penned fairy-tale.

How do you know whether you have found your true heart-wish or whether you have fallen victim to a bad compromise?

This question is not easy to answer because even if you do find your heart-wish you will always have to make *some* compromises for the simple reason that total perfection can't be found in the human world. For example, you might find your perfect house but it might not be of the right colour. You might find a gorgeous boyfriend but he might be living in the 'wrong' town. There are a thousand and one factors to each wish and I have not seen a single case where *all* these factors were perfectly matched to someone's wish. And even if they were, this perfect situation wouldn't last for long because everything is impermanent and changing all the time. (The only glorious exception to this rule is your own altruistic motivation, which can stay stable through every moment of your life and which is therefore the one and only reliable source of unconditional happiness.)

So, what you really need to learn is to distinguish a good compromise from a bad one. The following list will give you some clues as to how you can tell the two apart.

Good compromise	Bad compromise
The possibility that could be the fulfilment of your wish evokes the positive feelings in you that you wished for in your wish-list.	The possibility that could be the fulfilment of your wish looks very good but it *doesn't evoke the positive feelings* from your wish-list.
You see a few factors that aren't perfect but they don't diminish your positive feelings.	You see a few factors that aren't perfect and they make you feel really uncomfortable.
All the non-negotiable points from your wish-list are *fully* met.	Although this looks like a good opportunity, one or even two of your non-negotiable points from your wish-list are not fully met.
With this opportunity you can contribute to the world in the way you wished for.	With this opportunity you can't put your initial altruistic motivation into practice in the way you wanted.
None of the things you wanted to avoid is present in this opportunity.	You find one or even two of the points you wanted to avoid in this opportunity but you think that it doesn't matter. (Big risk!)

Let me give you a few examples. If you have found a gorgeous-looking boyfriend who has every quality you desire but you continue to feel like an ugly duckling when you are with him, you are about to make a bad compromise. But if you have found a boyfriend who looks totally different from what is actually 'your type', yet you feel wonderful with him and sexually attracted to him, you are about to make a good compromise. If he seems great and you feel wonderful with him but he has stood you up twice within your first week, you have a bad compromise again. It is important that you *feel really good* without ignoring any warning signs.

One last word of warning: avoiding bad compromises is not an excuse for doing nothing and becoming a burden on other people. If you can't find the job of your dreams straight away, you are doing yourself no favours if you don't work at all and become a nuisance to the people who have to support you financially, while you insist on 'not making a bad compromise'. The law of karma applies to every area of your life and if you make other people annoyed with you, you will end up with more problems instead of less.

It can be a *very good* compromise to have an awful job just to pay the bills while intensely working with wish-practice to find a better one. It can be a very good compromise as well to stay in one place for a while for the sake of the children, instead of moving every year because of your inner restlessness and frustration. Your wish-practice must never be an excuse not to be really caring for the people around you.

CHECK CAREFULLY WHETHER YOU HAVE FOUND YOUR HEART-WISH

Many people are fond of the idea that once they find their heart-wish they will have an immediate deep recognition of it and they will know straight away and beyond any doubt that they have finally achieved their aim. I totally agree that those love-at-first-sight feelings are wonderful and desirable. However, as nice as these feelings are, they can be highly deceitful as well. No matter how strongly you feel that you have found your dream, it is crucial to take a generous amount of time to check carefully whether this is really true. The above list of good and bad compromises can give you some clues, but as this relies a lot on your feelings, you need to give this test some time and to also *think* clearly whether you have found what you really wanted.

You can't rely solely on your intuition when checking whether your wish has come true.

Even people who work professionally as psychics have told me that they can't rely solely on their clairvoyant abilities when it comes to their own wishes. They all agree that our own intuition tends to get distorted when we are involved emotionally in a topic. This is because our desire and craving can be so strong that they can easily overpower the more subtle feelings of our intuition, which might tell us that things aren't quite as positive as we want them to be.

What seems to be a wonderful opportunity might just be a repetition of an old pattern that we have already wanted to give up for a long time. It isn't easy to break free from these old patterns and to withstand their enormous power to suck us again and again into their control. Nobody wants to repeat detrimental patterns but most of us do.

You only need to look at all the little negative habits you'd like to give up, such as always eating a whole bar of chocolate at once and always having too many commitments. If you realise how difficult it is to change even those small things you might understand how difficult it is to change stronger and more unconscious patterns. But don't worry – you can do it, everybody can – with the right amount of careful checking and unrelenting determination only to say 'Yes' to something that is really in alignment with your wish and to say 'No' to everything else. In order to make this decision you need to employ the intelligence of your heart (intuition), as well as the intelligence of your head (rationality).

In order to use your intuition you need to relax and to connect with your heart as well as you can, and then to check what you feel about the possible 'wish-fulfilment' that has been offered to you. If you feel an inner 'Yes' and a positive feeling, you might be on the right track. But then you need to use your head as well – you need to get out your initial wish-list and make sure that all of your non-negotiable points are *fully* met, and that all of the points you wanted to avoid are not present in this opportunity *at all*. Only when your heart *and* your head fully agree that you have found your heart-wish can you be sure that you have finally arrived at your aim.

DEAL WITH YOUR CHANGING RELATIONSHIPS

No matter what you wished for – if you are successful you will change and your relationships will have to change as well. Please don't expect that everybody around you will scream with delight once you have arrived at your wonderful aim. Unfortunately, many people will have mixed emotions when somebody in their midst suddenly becomes so much more successful and so much happier. Along with their joy for you they might well harbour some jealousy and some regret that they themselves are still stuck in the mud. If they have really strong negative feelings they might even break off contact with you. I have seen this happen.

Making big wishes come true is like going to another place in the universe and not everybody who is around you at the moment will want to come along. If you know that in advance you will be less shocked and hurt if it actually happens.

You might also feel a bit guilty if you become so much more successful than your friends or your family, and you might be painfully torn between your new exciting place in the universe and your cosy and familiar one among your old pals. However, you will not be able to relate to them in the same way as you did before if you have changed a lot. If you want to stay really close buddies with them *they* have to change as well. Unfortunately, they often don't.

The best insurance policy against painful changes in your relationships is to focus on how you want to contribute to the world with your wish. If your old friends and family feel that they are not excluded from your new-found freedom and fulfilment they will find it much easier to rejoice with you and to go on supporting you. If you are firmly rooted in your altruistic motivation, guilt feelings will rarely bother you, you will feel confident that you deserve what you have achieved and you will be able to share it freely with all your friends and family.

FINALLY – ENJOY THE RESULTS

You have worked so hard, you have been so patient and you were able to develop optimism and serenity against all the odds. Congratulations! Now is the time finally to enjoy the fulfilment of your wish.

If your altruistic motivation has been genuine and you are able to benefit others with the fulfilment of your aim, your joy will not wear off. You will not get used to your new-found fulfilment and you will not become rapidly dissatisfied. Instead you will stay deeply fulfilled.

This is what the Buddha and the spiritual leaders of all religions tried to bring across to us: that altruistic love is the answer to all our questions, the solution to all our problems and the remedy for all our illnesses. If you can feel this love in your heart and expand it by combining it with all of your present and future wishes you will stay happy for ever.

STEP 8, RECEIVING THE FULFILMENT OF YOUR WISH: THE ESSENTIALS

Step 8 is by far the best step of wish-practice because now you can finally receive the fulfilment of your wish. There are just some last pitfalls to avoid and then there hopefully will be nothing but roses and buttercups for you.

- Learn to discern bad from good compromises by listening to your heart *and* your head, and don't follow your auntie Mary's advice to settle for a 'sensible' solution that is only second best.

- Take your time and check carefully whether you have really arrived at your desired aim. Your intuition can easily be misleading when you are emotionally involved.

- Don't expect everybody to be rejoicing with delight when a mega-wish of yours has come true. If you change, your relationships may need to change as well.

- Finally – enjoy the results! If your altruistic motivation has been genuine and if you can continue to combine all your wishes with your intention to contribute to others you will be happy for ever.

ONE LAST NOTE

If you find wish-practice is working for you please don't hesitate to teach it to others. I'd love you to do that. The more people learn to bring their own personal wishes together with an altruistic motivation for others, the happier a world we will have. I am looking forward to it!